CHRISTIAN LIVING SERIES

~ Volume 1 ~

Christian Living Series

~ Volume 1 ~

Sacramental LIFE

by His Grace Bishop Youanis

ST SHENOUDA'S MONASTERY
SYDNEY, AUSTRALIA
2012

Christian Living Series - Volume 1
SACRAMENTAL LIFE

ST SHENOUDA MONASTERY
8419 Putty Rd,
Putty, NSW, 2330
Sydney, Australia

www.stshenoudamonastery.org.au

ISBN 13: 978-0-9873400-0-9

Cover Design:
Hani Ghaly,
Begoury Graphics
begourygraphics@gmail.com

Publisher's Note   7

About the Author   9

Preface   17

Introduction   21

The Life of Repentance   27

Confession   73

Holy Communion   111

Publisher's Note

✎

The four volumes of the Christian Living Series are the fruit of a catechism class that the late bishop Youanis used to teach to university students who came to Cairo from other states to study. The Chapters of these volumes have been a hand book for many Christians who are pursuing their spiritual path and a source of direction to many over the last fifty years, now we present it to you in the English language.

The Arabic edition of this book is originally titled "The Paradise of the Spirit" and contained more chapters yet we decided to bring you most of the chapters that were included in the original book and rearrange some of them for the spiritual benefit of the English readers. We would love to give a special thanks to those who laboured in the translation and proof reading of this book, who asked to remain anonymous. May the Lord reward them for their labour of love.

Volume one - SACRAMENTAL LIFE: Deals with the meaning and practical applications of two of the church sacraments. Chapters include: The life of Repentance, Confession, and Holy Communion.

Volume two - SPIRITUAL CONCEPTS: Explains some of the Christian concepts that are often misunderstood. Chapters include: Humility, Pride, Dignity, the Narrow gate, and the Life of submission.

Volume three - CHRISTIAN VIRTUES: Discusses some of the Christian Virtues that should accompany a Christian throughout their spiritual path. Chapters include: Purity, Prayer, Fasting, and Alms Giving.

Volume four - SPIRITUAL NOURISHMENTS: Prescribes the necessary Spiritual Nourishments that are needed along the spiritual path. Chapters include: Bible reading, Spiritual reading, Retreats, and Service.

About the Author

✿

HIS EARLY YEARS:

His Grace Bishop Youanis was born in the suburb of Shoubra, in Cairo, on the 25th of October 1923, from two pious parents.

In 1937, while in secondary school, he participated in Sunday School in Archangel Michael Church in Tosoun. In 1942, he became a servant in the same church. He was attached to the Sunday school house of "St Abu Makar." He was very active in his service as he also served in St Anthony and St Demiana Church in

Shoubra. In 1948, his Sunday school house of "St Abu Makar" moved to the El Farag suburb. There he joined Mr Nazeer Gayed (His Holiness Pope Shenouda) in the service of the class.

During his service in the house of Sunday School, he participated in producing a Sunday School magazine and used to write about the saints whom he loved.

He was called Ramzy Azouz and in 1952, he graduated from Cairo University with a Bachelor's degree in Faculty of Arts, History department. He worked as a history teacher in El Malek El Kamel school in Mansoura. During his work in Mansoura, he served the youth and interstate students who come to cairo to study. Many of them were attached to his grace until his departure.

IN THE DESERT OF SCETIES:

Mr Ramzy Azouz often went to the Virgin Mary's Monastery, El Syrian and used to spend summer holidays there since 1947. In the summer of 1955, he went to the monastery as usual and through divine direction and his love of the monastic life, the servant Ramzy Azouz chose to stay in the monastery to live a life of meditation. He was ordained a monk by the name of Fr Shenouda el Syriani, by Bishop Theophilos, the Abbot of the monastery.

FR SHENOUDA EL SYRIANI AND HIS VARIOUS FIELDS OF SERVICE:

Fr Shenouda el Syriani carried the cross of pain very early. When he entered the monastery, he suffered severe pain in the spinal cord that forced him to return to Cairo for treatment. This was a source of blessing to many for he began spiritually supervising the students at the theological college and continued to supervise them for many years. Many became his students and later priests in Cairo and other cities.

During this time, he was ordained a priest on 16/9/1956 by his grace Bishop Theophilios, the Abbot of the monastery. From then on, he became a father of confession and a spiritual advisor to many students of the clerical college.

Father Shenouda el Syriani was kind but also firm and strong for he treated the students of the Clerical College as both a father and teacher. He was preparing a generation of servants who would later become priests and fathers of the church.

Due to his various talents, he taught the subject of Spiritual Divinity. He wrote the first section of the Book "Garden of the Spirit" in 1960 which became a basic reference in spiritual life. He wrote the second part in 1963.

In spite his many duties of spiritual supervision and teaching in the Clerical College, he continued to spend long periods in the monastery. During his stay in the monastery, his Grace Bishop Theophilos gave him some duties to do:

• He became the abbot of the monastery

• He was in charge of meeting visitors, especially foreigners, as he was fluent in foreign languages

• He was in charge of cooperating with His Holiness

Pope Shenouda III (the monk Anthony el Syriani) and organising the monastery's library. There were large volumes of books and scrolls and he spent alot of effort indexing them.

• He co-operated with the monks to produce publications like the biography of St Basilus the great, an introduction to the book of Laws of Basilus, which was prepared for publication by His Holiness Pope Shenouda III. He also wrote many of the biographies that the monastery was publishing at that time like the biography of Mar Ephraim el Syriani and others.

During his time as a monk, he was a spiritual leader to many youth and servants. He was in charge of the retreat house of the monastery. The presence of Fr Shenouda el Syriani in the monastery motivated many to visit the monastery and enjoy a spiritual retreat. Many wanted to know the writer of the "Garden of the Spirit" Book.

His life in the monastery is well remembered by all the monks. His praying of the Holy Liturgy was special with its tune and spirituality. The monks still remember when he prayed the Holy Liturgy in Anba Bishoy's cell in El Syrian monastery on the day of his feast.

He loved the rites and used to teach the liturgy rites to the new monks whenever he was in the monastery.

IN THE SECRETARIAT OFFICE OF H.H. POPE KYROLLOS VI:

When the Lord chose Fr Mina to become Pope Kyrollos VI in 1959, fr Shenouda El Syriani was chosen by the Pope to become one of his four secretaries. He moved to the Patriarchate to continue to work hard in spite of his painful back. The caring Hand of the Lord was always supporting him.

In 1962, he became a hegumen by Bishop Theophilos, the Abbot of the monastery.

The late Pope Kyrollos delegated him in the first conference to represent the church in South Africa and Rodesia. He served in Sudan for a few months during this trip and the effects of his service are still felt to date.

Hegumen Shenouda continued working in spite of his severe pains. He had to travel to London in 1964 to have a surgical operation on his spinal cord. This dangerous operation was successful and he returned from London in 1965. His grace always surrendered his life to the Lord, who gave him years to continue his struggle in peace.

Hegumen Shenouda el Syriani returned to Cairo to teach the history of the church in the clerical college, besides his spiritual supervision of the students. He published books on the Christian Church in the Apostles' era, martyrdom in Christianity, Coptic Monasticism and the Church Councils.

BISHOP YOUANIS DURING THE TIME OF H.H. POPE SHENOUDA III:

When the Lord chose His Holiness Pope Shenouda to become the Patriarch on the see of St Mark, his holiness chose his colleague, Hegumen Shenouda el Syriani to become his secretary.

Pope Shenouda became the Patriarch on 14 November 1971 and the first Bishop to be ordained by him was his grace Bishop Youanis, Bishop of el Garbiya on 12 December 1971.

Bishop Youanis was gifted with many talents, and hence Pope Shenouda gave him many important tasks that concerned the management of the church as a whole:

• He was in charge of the secretariat of the Holy Synod in 1972 and continued in this role for 12 years in addition to his other duties.

• He was the president of the clerical council.

• He was a member of the Coptic buildings association (waaf)

• He also communicated with the Catholic Church on local and international levels.

• He accompanied His Holiness in his historical trips to the Vatican in 1973, the USA in 1977 and Sudan in 1979.

• He represented the Coptic Church in international meetings on the Middle Eastern Council of Churches level, the International Council of Churches and meetings of the Orthodox Churches.

• He was delegated by His Holiness to manage the church affairs during the Pope's trip to Armenia and Russia in 1972.

• His Holiness asked him to visit the French bishops before accepting them in the church. He presented a detailed report to His Holiness and afterwards these Bishops became part of the church.

• He obtained the relics of the great apostle St Paul

in December 1973 and they were kept in a suitable place in St Paul's Cathedral in Tanta.

HIS PASTORAL ACHIEVEMENTS IN THE DIOCESE OF ELGARBIYA:

• During his time, he ordained 34 priests for different cities in the Diocese, 14 of them for Tanta.

• Six new churches were built with the most famous being St Paul's Cathedral.

• Two other churches were bought from other denominations and five of the churches were totally renovated.

• He renovated the Patriarchate and built a large building adjacent to it that contained a big reception hall and many rooms for various activities.

• He built a home for the consecrated sisters in front of St Paul's Cathedral.

• During his time a branch of the theological college was opened in Tanta in 1976 and later an institution for service and another for church hymns were joined to it.

• He felt the importance of teaching his congregation and so he conducted a general meeting every Friday and added another meeting on Sunday during the forty days of fasting at St Mark's Cathedral in Tanta, and another meeting in el Mahala el Kobra city every Thursday.

• He looked after the villages' service in all the cities of the diocese and established more than 30 altars in different villages.

• He restored the old monastery of St Mina in Ebiar and opened a hospitality home in the monastery in 1980.

• He established a centre for visual and hearing aids in the diocese.

• During his time, he produced 15 publications.

HIS DEPARTURE:

On Wednesday, 4th of November 1987 at 1:00pm, after a long battle, our beloved Bishop Youanis departed and his spirit returned to the heavenly dwelling carried by the angels. He looked angelic while lying on his bed and his hands were white as snow. On Thursday, 5th of November, his holiness along with 20 Bishops prayed and farewelled his pure body in the presence of thousands of his sons and all those who loved him from all over the country.

We farewell our beloved father to the glory and continue feeling his presence in his pleasant biography and through all his work.

Preface

x

This book is an outcome of spiritual struggle from the beginning to the end. This is the spiritual struggle that the apostle mentioned: "For to you it has been granted on behalf of Christ, not only to believe in Him, but also to suffer for His sake." (Phil 1:29) This is the period when I returned to the world from the monastery as a result of my sickness. I ended up working in the Clerical College at Anba Reweis where I taught the subject of "Spiritual Divinity" besides the spiritual supervision of the students.

Four years ago, when I started teaching this subject, I could not find any books that dealt with the Christian virtues in detail. I desired to teach students the Christian virtues precisely, not just in simple or abstract form.

Just last year, I had to leave the monastery and return to the world to be treated from an acute health problem where I was confined in bed for about two and a half months. This last period was a great blessing for I wrote the book in its final format as you are reading now. At the time, I felt the Grace of God assisting my weakness.

I thank God from the bottom of my heart for I felt that His right Hand was holding my hand in all that I wrote. Yes I felt Him in every stage of the book.

I also thank the Lord for the Grace that filled one of His honest servants – Bishop Theophilos, Bishop and Abbot of the Virgin's monastery (El Syrian) who contributed in the development of the monastic life in this mountain. He supplied the library with hundreds of books. He obtained writings of the Church's fathers from both American and European libraries. Thus it is fair to say that this book is also a fruit of this great Bishop. May the Lord preserve his life for the glory of His blessed Name.

I also give thanks to the Lord for my fathers, the monks of El Syrian monastery who supported me by their prayers and guidance. One particular father participated in the production of this book in its current picture, whether by his writings or his guidance. It was appropriate to mention his name but he refused, denying himself; may the Lord reward him and write his name in the Book of eternal life.

I also cannot forget to thank our teacher, Dr Wahib Attallah who reviewed the book in spite of his many duties.

I put this humble book in the Hands of our Lord who loves us and I ask Him that it becomes a blessing for everyone who reads it. I also beseech the grace of the Lord to help me produce the second and third book of this series.

May the Lord be glorified in our weakness and to Him be all glory forever. Amen

Father Shenouda el Syriani
14 July 1960 } The commemoration of the
7 Abib 1676 } departure of St Shenouda

Introduction

Every work has an aim directing its path. The aim of this book, my brother, is your salvation, as we want you to work for it and desire it. We also know that in your spiritual struggle, you need to avoid some things and to acquire others. You need to avoid sin and find out its cause, whether it be from the outside environment, your inner desires, wars from the world, the devil or the inability of the soul to stand firm in front of all these.

In this book, we do not want to close our eyes on some things and forget the truth. We will picture ourselves as we really are: a person who has desires and faces various wars. We are all weak and have not reached this higher spiritual level. So we will not attempt high spiritual stages initially. Our way is to take you step by step in order to grow spiritually without unnecessary laps. Sometimes these laps in the spiritual life can be dangerous and have an opposite effect.

THE STARTING POINT:

Where do we start? We will start from the beginning of the road, from the life of repentance. Repentance is a good start for all of us. It is the turning point in any life, to leave sin and walk with God. Who does not sin? "All are like sheep going astray, each one to his own way." The world attracts us and tempts us to follow like drunken people, not feeling what we are doing. However, we finally wake up and realise our drastic faults and feel apologetic. We want to live a new life with God, a life of purity. We cry with David saying: "I lay down and slept, I awoke for the Lord sustained me." This waking is the beginning of repentance.

Some of us wake up and realise the need to have someone as a guide, along the steps of the road. Others have not woken up and are still asleep in ignorance and pleasure. Others have partly woken up, realised their sins, yet are struggling to repent. Others are struggling within themselves and need someone to guide them to repentance. However, others do not want to wake up. They do not realise that they are asleep. Haughtiness is a barrier between them and repentance as they do not want to confess that they are sinners.

Let us suppose, our beloved brother, that you have awaken from ignorance and pleasure. What next? What is the new life and its way? How can a person repent? How can he keep his repentance? How can he grow in repentance and have fruits? With the grace of God, we will detail the steps of the way.

STEPS OF THE WAY:

The first thing that worries a repentant person is his old sins. He thinks of how to get rid of the burden of sins that torments him. Thus "confession" is the first step in repentance as a repentant person feels at ease when his sins are forgiven. Next comes the additional step of "partaking of the Lord's body and blood" which gives a Godly power to help one stay firm on the way. Consequently, we had to write two separate subjects on confession and communion, where we explained these two great sacraments and their practice in the life of repentant people. We explained their requisites, fruits and other related questions.

With confession and communion, a sinner will enter the church repentant. What about the new life that he will live after his repentance? What are the basics? Here, the spiritual life needs humility so we wrote a chapter on humbleness, and explained its importance and meaning. We also discussed two related topics, pride and worldly dignity.

After the basics, we needed to start building. We started with the life of purity, for the sin of adultery is the second most dangerous sin that can destroy one's spiritual life, after the sin of pride. We then wrote about anger, a common sin. We talked about the sins of the tongue and started by mentioning the proper manner of speech and silence. We mentioned general sins of the tongue and discussed the sin of judging others, another common weakness.

Thus we have covered repentance and its strength through confession and communion. We also covered common sins that hinder repentance like pride, adultery, anger and sins of the tongue. What about after the building? In the two remaining sections of the Garden of the Spirit, we will discuss virtues, their practices and general aspects of spiritual life.

THIS BOOK IS NOT FOR ME:

I can hear someone whispering: "This book is not for me. Why should I learn about the life of repentance? This is for beginners; as for me I have passed this stage from a long time and all these issues I have learnt from my youth. I want to read about higher stages: visions, dreams, talents and Godly love!"

My brother, thinking this way is dangerous as repentance is not a stage that a person can pass, it is a way of life. As long as we sin, we need to repent. The kind of sin may vary as the individual matures spiritually but every day we need to resist sin, for our fight will never end as long as we are in the world and in our bodies. So if you do not sin, my brother, then truly this book is not for you. It is for human beings who sinned and are sinning.

To desire higher levels of spirituality is dazzling for some people. However, you need to remember that a building starts from the bottom and not from the top. It is good to long for these levels but you must climb from the bottom foundation, which is repentance. Beware lest this desire for spiritual elevation is a result of some pride still hidden within yourself. While you were a sinner, you desired to be great in earthly matters and now while you are on the road of the Holy City, you desire to also be great but in spiritual form!

Be humble my brother, for you cannot reach the level of the saints and their talents in one jump. They did not reach what they achieved except through hard labour, tears, and much falling and rising. They did not reach a total work of grace in their lives except after the grace of God left them for times on their own, to realise their weak nature and the strength of their enemy. They confessed their inability in front of the Lord and in front of people and bowed their heads to the ground, and then the grace of God crowned them with many crowns. Thus grace lived in them and gave them many talents, confident that they will not be affected by pride as they know their weak selves, remembering their many falls. As for us, my brother, we cannot receive the crowns of the saints while our heads are feeling high and strong. Let us first weep on our sins, and be sad that Jerusalem's fence is broken and its gates are burnt. Let us first live a life of repentance and be totally humble. Let us always feel that we are beginners and check ourselves carefully, feeling sorry for any sin or wrong doing or idle thought. Let us say we are not worthy of the Lord's talents and are not qualified for higher spiritual levels.

Let us live like that my brother, and then the grace of God will come and visit us and work within us, so we will rejoice by its work and not ours, and thus give glory to God Almighty.

Goodbye until we meet in the next part of the Book.

A monk from El Syrian Monastery

The Life of Repentance

🕊

"But unless you repent, you will all likewise perish"

(Lk 13: 5)

- ❦ What is Sin?
- ❦ What does sin do?
- ❦ What does repentance do?
- ❦ The merciful God whom we worship
- ❦ How do I repent?
- ❦ Characteristics of a repentant person
- ❦ Questions and Answers
- ❦ Examples of repentant people
- ❦ What the fathers said about about repentance

WHAT IS SIN?

God created man pure and saintly in His own countenance and image. However due to man's rebellion against the Creator and his fall into sin, his nature changed and he lost his rank in Paradise where he used to enjoy the presence of God. This led to a loss of peace, joy and authority over other creatures. Only sin and its consequences remained for him. Man was unclothed of the robe of glory and suffered from the coldness of iniquity as He willingly distanced himself from the Sun of Righteousness. He lost His warmth, and was deprived from seeing light and brightness.

Therfore, sin is a violation and rebellion against God and His commandment. It is death itself as the Lord Jesus refers to the Prodigal Son saying, "…..was dead and is alive again, was lost and is found." (Lk 15: 32)

Sin is weakness, defeat and failure because one who falls in sin cannot control himself, but rather yields to the authority of sin and its slavery.

WHAT DOES SIN DO?

WORRY AND LOSS OF PEACE:

As a result of sin, man lost his peace and inherited worry instead. Thus worry is connected to sin, it comes and settles when we sin, and makes a person lose his inner peace which comes from God. As mentioned by the Apostle, peace guards a person's heart and mind"...and the peace of God, which surpasses all understanding, will guard your hearts and minds through Christ Jesus." (Phil 4: 7). Isaiah the Prophet says: "But the wicked are like the troubled sea, when it cannot rest, whose waters cast up mire and dirt. "There is no peace,"says my God, "for the wicked." (Isa 57: 20-21). How profound is the Prophet's words about a wicked person "he cannot rest." Even if he wants to rest he cannot because peace is a fruit of the Holy Spirit (Gal. 5: 22). David the Prophet Describes his feelings when he was in sin saying, "There is no soundness in my flesh because of Your anger, nor any health in my bones" (Ps 38: 3).

A wicked person has an adversary who is always fighting and distressing him until he repents. This adversary is his conscious which, according to the interpretation of the fathers, our Lord Christ ordered us to reconcile with, "Agree with your adversary quickly, while you are on the way with him." (Mt 5: 25). For example, after Cain killed his brother, Abel, he cried out to God saying, "I shall be hidden from Your face; I shall be a fugitive and a vagabond on the earth, and it will happen that anyone who finds me will kill me...." And the Lord set a mark on Cain, lest anyone finding him should kill him." (Gen 4: 14-15). This mark increased Cain's remorse...!!

So long as a person is far from God, he is always living in worry and anxiety until he comes back to Him, finding complete rest and relief. Similarly, the dove sent out by Noah, returned back to the ark when it could not find rest in the world. Moreover, when Jonah resisted God, the waves and the winds of the sea kept pestering him, until he returned to God through prayer inside the belly of the great fish.

We read of criminals and offenders who initially escaped the grip of police, yet willingly surrendered themselves to the police after many years and confessed their crimes. This is because they preferred confession and punishment over pangs of remorse.

Actually, nothing can steal one's inner peace more than sin… Job lost his cattle, cows, camels, servants and all his children in one day, yet his calamity was not as severe as David's when he sinned! Job's temptation did not deprive him of his peace, as he said, "Naked I came from my mother's womb, and naked shall I return there. The Lord gave, and the Lord has taken away; Blessed be the name of the Lord." (Job 1:21), while poor David said after his sin,"I wet my bed with my tears" and "…my sin is always before me."

GRIEF AND DEPRESSION:

Grief and depression always accompany sin as they are the fruits of sin, while joy is a fruit of the Holy Spirit. During the Babylon captivity, the Israelites were surrounded by beautiful willow trees, yet they never forgot the bitterness of captivity. They mixed their tears with the waters of the river. Instead of singing, they wept and cried. Instead of playing music, they hung up their harps, as there was no room for Joy. "By the rivers of Babylon, there we sat and wept when we remembered Zion. We hung our harps on the willows in the midst of it." (Ps 137:

1) This Psalm reminds us of the soul's 'spiritual captivity,' being captured by Satan and held away from Jerusalem, the city of the Great King (Mt 5: 35) It reminds us of life in Babylon, a city of adulterers (Rev 14:8,18:2).

HOPLESSNESS:

The fruit of grief and depression might grow, carrying the poison of death and leading to hoplessness, loss of faith, and suicide. The highest percentage of suicidal rates are in developed countries, where permissiveness is a good soil for sin.

BAD RELATIONSHIPS WITH PEOPLE:

While sin deprives us of our peace and good relationship with God, it has the same effect on other people. If love is the bond of perfection, sin is the contrary, because sin is a transgression, "Whoever commits sin also commits lawlessness, and sin is lawlessness." (1 Jn 3: 4). It is transgression to the Lord's commandments and also to others. What could we say about a thief, an attacker and an adulterer? Isn't this considered an encroachment against other people?

SIN ATTRACTS THE WRATH OF GOD:

As a result of sin, God cursed the earth which He had created in perfection. After the fall, He said to Adam, "Cursed is the ground for your sake." (Gen 3: 17) As a result of sin, God burnt Sodom and Gomorrah, despite

Abraham's intercession on their behalf, "and did not spare the ancient world, but saved Noah, one of eight people, a preacher of righteousness, bringing in the flood on the world of the ungodly; and turning the cities of Sodom and Gomorrah into ashes, condemned them to destruction, making them an example to those who afterward would live ungodly." (2 Pet 2: 5-6)

Sin led to the destruction of 23,000 Israelites after they committed adultery with the daughters of Moab. (1 Cor 10: 8) If sin was not dreadful, then why did David cry day and night and wet his bed with bitter tears?! Sin deprives us from the support of our Mighty Lord. For example, God abandoned the children of Israel when they were defeated in the small city of Ai because of the sin of Achan, the son of Carmi. (Joshua 7) Sin separates us from God and stops our cries from reaching Him, "Behold, the Lord's hand is not shortened that it cannot save; nor His ear heavy, that it cannot hear. But your iniquities have separated you from your God; and your sins have hidden His face from you, so that He will not hear." (Isa 59: 1-2)

David the Prophet also says: "If I regard iniquity in my heart, the Lord will not hear." (Ps 66: 18), Therefore, sin prevents us from receiving gifts from God. "Your iniquities have turned these things away, and your sins have withheld good from you." (Jer 5: 25)

SIN BRINGS FORTH SHAME AND ILLNESS:

Sin brings forth shame and failure to a human soul, "Righteousness exalts a nation, but sin is a reproach to people." (Prov 14: 34) To test the power of these words, consider the reproach of adulterers, drunkards, and addicts.

In addition, sin adds illness to our body, as declared by our Lord Jesus Christ when He healed the man with an infirmity for 38 years, "Afterward Jesus found him in the temple, and said to him, "See, you have been made well. Sin no more, lest a worse thing come upon you." (Jn 5: 14)

SIN BRINGS FORTH FEAR:

Sin humiliates a person and brings forth fear (Rev 21: 8) and shame (Gen 2: 25, Prov 31: 5). It makes us lose control over ourselves and enslaves us to bad habits. Sin also makes us fear the least harmful creatures and the weakest animals. Before Adam sinned in Paradise, he lived in harmony among wild beasts as they subdued to him in complete obedience, since God gave this authority. (Gen 1: 26) However, Man willingly gave up this authority by sinning. Yet, through a life of repentance, we can reach the state of righteousness that was attained before the fall. We hear of many saints who lived and befriended wild beasts.

WHAT DOES REPENTANCE DO?

Repentance is the message of Christianity. John the Baptist, who paved the way before Christ, called all people to repent (Mk 1:4). The Lord Jesus Himself preached about repentance, and advised His disciples to repent as the Kingdom of God is at hand.

The word 'metania' is a Greek word which means repentance. To be more linguistically accurate, it means a change of heart and life. This is clear in St. Paul's words, "Therefore, if anyone is in Christ, he is a new creation; old things have passed away; behold, all things have become new." (2 Cor 5: 17). Christianity calls for the newness of everything, "No one puts a piece of unshrunk cloth on an old garment; for the patch pulls away from the garment, and the tear is made worse. Nor do they put new wine into old wineskins, or else the wineskins break, the wine is spilled, and the wineskins are ruined. But they put new wine into new wineskins, and both are preserved." (Mt 9: 16-17)

The saints understand repentance as a reconciliation with God, a second baptism, a purification of iniquities, a waving of sins or a means of returning to God…. Repentance amends what sin has spoiled, and builds what disobedience has demolished. It renews the hearts of sinners and clothes them in righteousness. It casts away the works of darkness and powers of the devils. It cures and resurrects those who have died spiritually because of sin. It is like a sea cleansing all the sinners and purifying them. It drags sinners from the streets and takes them into heaven…

When we sin, we lose all spiritual gifts, virtues and blessings, but repentance restores them all back to us. The way of repentance is a safe one and it opens the gates for God's kind bosom, "…and the one who comes to Me, I will by no means cast out." (Jn 6:37)

THE MERCIFUL GOD
WHOM WE WORSHIP

Mercy and salvation are directly related to forgiveness. It is only because of God's Mercy that we have forgiveness and our repentance is accepted. I repent to gain forgiveness of my sins, but if God does not forgive, what is the use of repentance?!

Wouldn't forgiving my sins contradict these words, "For the wages of sin is death" (Rom 6: 23). This would have been the case if God had not interfered with His Mercy. Mercy proceeds the justice of God, as explained by David the Prophet, "Surely His salvation is near to those who fear Him, that glory may dwell in our land. Mercy and truth have met together; Righteousness and peace have kissed." (Ps 85: 9-10).

The mercy of God didn't contradict His justice nor decline His work, but it found a solution for sinners; being the act of redemption. God being the unlimited, incarnated in the form of a human being to redeem man who deserved unlimited punishment as a result of disobeying God's unlimited commandments. No angel, archangel or prophet or anybody could have accomplished this salvation.

PROPHETS AND APOSTLES DECLARE GOD'S MERCY:

Repentance depends on God's mercy as He is aware of the weaknesses of human beings. The Holy Bible assures us: "And the Lord passed before him and proclaimed, "The

Lord, the Lord God, merciful and gracious, longsuffering, and abounding in goodness and truth, keeping mercy for thousands, forgiving iniquity and transgression and sin." (Ex 34: 6, 7)

As in Psalm 103, David, the great Psalmist remembers the Lord's unlimited grace and mercy. For this, he urges his soul to honour the Lord. In another Psalm, "The Lord is gracious and full of compassion, slow to anger and great in mercy. The Lord is good to all, and His tender mercies are over all His works. (Ps145: 8, 9)

David keeps praising God's mercy until it becomes more important than life itself, "Because Your loving kindness is better than life, my lips shall praise You."(Ps 63: 3)

However, Jonah the Prophet was upset with God's mercy as God granted salvation to the city of Nineveh after Jonah warned them of the destruction of their wicked deeds; "So he prayed to the Lord, and said, "Ah, Lord, was not this what I said when I was still in my country? Therefore I fled previously to Tarshish; for I know that You are a gracious and merciful God, slow to anger and abundant in lovingkindness, One who relents from doing harm." (Jon 4: 2), Therefore, the great mercies of the Lord became a subject of meditation for the men of God, "This I recall to my mind, therefore I have hope. Through the Lord's mercies we are not consumed, because His compassions fail not. They are new every morning; Great is Your faithfulness." (Lam 3: 21-23)

In the New Testament, the Apostles highlight God's mercy and our free salvation as it is an era of redemption, salvation and grace. The whole idea of salvation depends on God's mercy. If it wasn't for His mercy, there wouldn't be any redemption or salvation. He loves us because of His great mercy; as is clear in all writings of the New Testament.

Zachariah, the father of St. John the Baptist, after being filled with the Holy Spirit said, "And you, child, will be called the prophet of the Highest; for you will go before the face of the Lord to prepare His ways, to give knowledge of salvation to His people by the remission of their sins, through the tender mercy of our God, with which the Dayspring from on high has visited us" (Lk 1: 76-78).

St. Paul says, "But God, who is rich in mercy, because of His great love with which He loved us, even when we were dead in trespasses, made us alive together with Christ (by grace you have been saved)," (Eph. 2: 4-5). Also, "not by works of righteousness which we have done, but according to His mercy He saved us, through the washing of regeneration and renewing of the Holy Spirit" (Titus 3: 5).

St. Peter the Apostle mentions, "Blessed be the God and Father of our Lord Jesus Christ, who according to His abundant mercy has begotten us again to a living hope through the resurrection of Jesus Christ from the dead" (1 Pet 1: 3).

THE MERCIFUL GOD PROMISED FORGIVENESS FOR THE REPENTANT:

We can assuredly say that we are now in the age

of mercy... a mercy which tolerated humiliation and sufferings up till death. So, let's come to Him repenting, regretting, confessing and announcing our sins and iniquities, yet believing His promise.   He is always stretching His arms and calling out to everyone, "Come to Me, all you who labour and are heavy laden, and I will give you rest" (Mt 11: 28), and, "the one who comes to Me, I will by no means cast out." (Jn 6: 37).

He is ready to forget our sins and cast them in the sea of forgetfulness. "Who is a God like You, pardoning iniquity and passing over the transgression of the remnant of His heritage? He does not retain His anger forever, because He delights in mercy. He will again have compassion on us, and will subdue our iniquities. He will cast all our sins into the depths of the sea." (Mic 7:18-19)

How numerous are the promises of God which encourage us to come back to Him and repent. He promises to forget all our previous sins and become through Him and with Him, a new creation. The Lord says through Ezekiel the Prophet: "But if a wicked man turns from all his sins which he has committed, keeps all My statutes, and does what is lawful and right, he shall surely live; he shall not die. None of the transgressions which he has committed shall be remembered against him; because of the righteousness which he has done, he shall live. Do I have any pleasure at all that the wicked should die?" says the Lord GOD, "and not that he should turn from his ways and live? "But when a righteous man turns away from his righteousness and commits iniquity, and does according to all the abominations that the wicked man does, shall he live? All the righteousness which he has done shall not be remembered; because of the unfaithfulness of which he is guilty and the sin which he has committed, because of them he shall die." (Ezek 18: 21-24)

Also in the Book of Isaiah, "Seek the Lord while He may be found, call upon Him while He is near. Let the wicked forsake his way, and the unrighteous man his thoughts; Let him return to the Lord, and He will have mercy on him; and to our God, for He will abundantly pardon." (Isa 55:6)

St. Peter says: "Repent therefore and be converted, that your sins may be blotted out, so that times of refreshing may come from the presence of the Lord," (Acts 3: 19). Also, "The Lord is not slack concerning His promise, as some count slackness, but is longsuffering toward us, not willing that any should perish but that all should come to repentance." (2 Pet 3: 9)

The precious stones in the crown which our Lord places on the heads of the repentant, announce God's great Mercy and His continuous call for repentance.

For example, Luke 15 proclaims, "Then all the tax collectors and the sinners drew near to Him to hear Him. And the Pharisees and scribes complained, saying, "This Man receives sinners and eats with them." So He spoke this parable to them, saying..." (Lk 15: 1-3). At this point, the Lord mentioned three parables, The Lost Sheep, the Lost Coin and the Lost Son; all highlight the Lord's deep love for sinners and His wait for their repentance and return.

THE PARABLE OF THE LOST SON:

The son who left his father's house is an example of those who leave God and His House. This son journeyed to a far country, and wasted his possessions with prodigal living. But when he had spent all, there arose a severe famine in that land, and he began to be in want. He joined himself to a citizen of that country, who sent him into his fields to feed swine. The Lost son would gladly fill his stomach with the pods that the swine ate, as no one gave him anything to eat; These are all consequences of sin and its aftermath. When he came back to himself, he decided to rise and go to his father asking for forgiveness, a sign of repentance and regret. The Lord Jesus says, "And he arose and came to his father. But when he was still a great way off, his father saw him and had compassion, and ran and fell on his neck and kissed him." (Lk 15:20). How wonderful are these words pointing to the great love and kindness of God towards the sinners!!

"But when he was still a great way off, his father saw him and had compassion..." These words declare that his father was waiting!! If this is the case with the physical father, what about the Heavenly Father's feelings and emotions towards His beloved children. Our Lord reproaches us in another verse, "If you then, being evil, know how to give good gifts to your children, how much more will your Father who is in heaven give good things to those who ask Him!" (Mt 7: 11)

Then what did the father do when he saw his Prodigal Son? "His father saw him and had compassion, and ran and fell on his neck and kissed him." That was what the father did before hearing any apology from his son. It is a bit strange that the father ran, while it is the son who should have run; but it is great love which forgets any offences or misbehaviour. What about the great love of God for His children who have left Him and listened to the enemy? Wouldn't He have mercy on them, unbind them from any bondages and set them free? The Lord says: "Those who are well have no need of a physician, but those who are sick. For I did not come to call the righteous, but sinners, to repentance." (Mt 9: 12-13)

Now, what about the son, what did he do? When he was in the far country he promised himself, "I will arise and go to my father, and will say to him, "Father, I have sinned against heaven and before you, and I am no longer worthy to be called your son. Make me like one of your hired servants." When he went back to his father, he said these words, but the father didn't allow him to say the last sentence "Make me like one of your hired servants". This point is very important as it highlights the close relationship we should have with God. We can never lose our Sonship to our Heavenly Father, no matter how grievous our sins are. This is why our church does not repeat a baptism after someone has denied the faith, and later returned to Christianity.

We should never forget that we are God's children to whom He sacrificed His Precious Blood, "knowing that you were not redeemed with corruptible things, like silver or gold, from your aimless conduct received by tradition from your fathers, but with the precious blood of Christ, as of a lamb without blemish and without spot." (1 Pet 1:18-19)

The word 'Our Father' is so sweet in God's ears. He

loves to hear us calling Him. That is why He ordered His disciples to say, "Our Father Who art in Heaven…" (Lk 11: 2)

Then what happened after the Prodigal Son repented and offered an apology? The father ordered, 'Bring out the best robe and put it on him, and put a ring on his hand and sandals on his feet. And bring the fatted calf here and kill it, and let us eat and be merry; for this my son was dead and is alive again; he was lost and is found.' The son was naked because of sin (Gen 3: 7) and his father clothed him. That is the work of repentance; it clothes the sinner with the robe of righteousness. The question here is: Was not the elder son who always lived with his father worthy of this robe?? Yet, it is the mercy of the father, for the sick son needs more attention than the healthy siblings. Similarly the sick in spirit needs more love and kindness.

The ring put on his hand is a symbol of the covenant between the father and his son, so he would never return to his wrong doings. The father put a lot of care into clothing his son and making him look original again, as though he had done nothing wrong.

The son only offered his father some apologetic words, but the father bestowed on him great things. The same could be said about our relationship with our Heavenly Father. We can just offer Him our repentance, apology, regret and tears and He will accept us. He will pour out His goodness and replace all spiritual gifts we lost through sin. See the unutterable great mercies, kindness and love of Our Lord!! Although we insult, tease and blasphemy His blessed Name, He still works for our salvation!!

How Do I Repent?

Give Self Account of Your Deeds:

The first step in repentance is to give a self-account. Sit alone and think about what you have done, just like the Prodigal Son. Remember your weariness and loss of inner peace. Tell yourself: How many of my (Heavenly) father's hired servants have bread (spiritual gifts) enough to spare and I perish with hunger (spiritually)! Where is my Joy? What is the result of my sinful way of life?

If you are honest with yourself, you will stand in reverence before the Lord, offering true prayer from the depth of your heart. You will be ashamed; facing the floor, weeping and beating your chest, saying with the Prodigal son, "Father I have sinned against Heaven and before You." This is the main base of the spiritual life, about which the saints talked a lot. We might be ashamed to open up with others, but not with ourselves. We might get tired of people's advices and instructions, but our inner self will never get tired when we beat our chests and be strict with ourselves.

Giving an account of our deeds also revives the virtues which may have become lukewarm, as a result of our sins.

An Example:

If you have an anger problem, try to recall what made you so angry? What did the other person say to initiate your anger? Should you have interpreted his words in a more simple way of understanding? Why didn't you tolerate him although he said these harsh words? Why shouldn't you follow the Lord's steps in tolerating insult and reproach? Are you a good disciple of the Lord? Doesn't He say, "Very truly I tell you, no servant is greater than his master, nor is a messenger greater than the one who sent him." (Jn 13:16). You then realise that the reason for your anger was your lack of love towards that person. As a result, you become more loving and patient next time.

The aim of this self-account is to treat your weaknesses and fight falling into sin. As the apostle says, "See then that you walk circumspectly, not as fools but as wise." (Eph 5:15)

WARNING:

When remembering your sins during repentance, beware of the devil's snares. He can attract you again to your old memories and revive your desires, especially with sins related to anger, envy, vain glory and sexual issues. For this reason, our church always prays in the Holy Liturgy: "Cleanse us from all blemish, all guile, all hypocrisy, all malice and the remembrance of evil entailing death." So as soon as you notice the beginning of this war, direct your thoughts to something different and don't give the devil a chance.

For the benefit of spiritual growth, the best time for self-account is:

• Straight after falling into a sin, to offer repentance and regret.

• At the end of each day, getting ready for a fresh

start the next day.

- Before having confession with your confession father.

- At the end of each week. Just as you consider physical rest during the weekend, consider spiritual rest and revival too.

- At the end of each year. If God has given you grace, supported and sustained you this year, you should cry out, "You crown the year with Your goodness, and Your paths drip with abundance." (Ps 65: 11) If you are living in an ungodly manner, remember these words, "And even now the axe is laid to the root of the trees. Therefore every tree which does not bear good fruit is cut down and thrown into the fire." (Mt 3: 10)

Plead to the Lord saying, "Sir, let it alone this year also..." (Lk 13: 8). St. Gregory the theologian mentioned that in early Christianity the people used to give a yearly self-account on the feast of Epiphany, renewing their promise to the Lord on the day of their baptism.

Whether you are confessing your sins, asking for help or thanking God for His grace and sustenance, you should always raise your heart to the Lord in REPENTANCE and Thanksgiving.

Sin humiliates God and arouses His wrath. It separates us from Him, deprives us of our peace and adds to our weariness. If it wasn't the case, why did the saints weep for their sins? Look at David the Prophet and King in Psalm 6 as he repeats that his sins were ever before him. But as for us, we don't care about our sins. Whenever we feel choked and depressed, we entertain ourselves with temporary and artificial means of comfort...

Try to remember your sins and ignorance. Your tears wash away your iniquities. St John Chrysostom says: "If you remember your sins, God will forget them, but if you forget them, God never does."

REST AND SALVATION IN CHRIST ONLY:

Be sure that true peace and rest are in Christ only, as he says: "Come to Me, all you who labour and are heavy laden, and I will give you rest" (Mt 11: 28). He gave His disciples His complete peace, a holy gift which surpasses all the worldly gifts; "Peace I leave with you, My peace I give to you; not as the world gives do I give to you." (Jn 14: 27)

Always put in your heart that getting rid of sin and its authority is only through Christ. Believe in His name, power and support, and have great hope in His Mercy. Use the means of salvation set by our church, "Nor is there salvation in any other, for there is no other name under heaven given among men by which we must be saved." (Acts 4: 12). No matter how hard we try, if we depend on our self, we will fail, as Lord Jesus says, "...for without Me you can do nothing." (Jn 15: 5). Remember the Psalmist words, "Unless the Lord builds the house, they labour in vain who build it; Unless the Lord guards the city, the watchman stays awake in vain." (Ps 127: 1)

MEDITATE ON THE VANITY OF THIS WORLD:

Make sure you know that the world is vain. Use the world and don't let it use you. Live in it but don't allow it to live within your heart. Where are all the great kings and emperors who lived before you in this world? They are in the graves and you can never distinguish between the bones of a great king and his servants, the erudite and the ignorant…

Beware of getting too occupied with the vain glories of the world. Beware of drifting off the path of your salvation. Do not postpone your repentance. Do not get enchanted with the glare of the world because that is how Satan tried to tempt the Lord Jesus, "Again, the devil took Him up on an exceedingly high mountain, and showed Him all the kingdoms of the world and their glory. And he said to Him, "All these things I will give You if You will fall down and worship me." Then Jesus said to him, "Away with you, Satan! For it is written, 'You shall worship the Lord your God, and Him only you shall serve." (Mt 4: 10)

KNOW YOUR SELF-WORTH :

You would never ignore your salvation if you remind yourself of the value of your soul. It is the most precious thing in the whole world, as the Lord says: "For what profit is it to a man if he gains the whole world, and loses his own soul? Or what will a man give in exchange for his soul?" (Mt 16: 26)

The price of your soul is the precious blood of the Lord Jesus Christ… it is very strange that some people care a lot about cleaning their body and clothes, but are reluctant to clean their souls. My dear brethren we are in the age of mercy, but hereafter in heaven, we will be in the age of justice. If you humiliate justice here you can resort to mercy, but if you humiliate mercy who will you resort to hereafter?!

DO NOT POSTPONE REPENTANCE:

Never postpone repentance, for many of those in Hades postponed repentance. Death didn't give them the chance to repent and came when they never expected it!!

Beware of resembling the foolish virgins hearing the Master's Voice, "I do not know you." (Mt 25: 11), or the rich man about whom the Lord Jesus says, "Then He spoke a parable to them, saying: "The ground of a certain rich man yielded plentifully, and he thought within himself, saying, 'What shall I do, since I have no room to store my crops?' So he said, 'I will do this: I will pull down my barns and build greater, and there I will store all my crops and my goods. And I will say to my soul, "Soul, you have many goods laid up for many years; take your ease; eat, drink, and be merry."' But God said to him, 'Fool! This night your soul will be required of you; then whose will those things be which you have provided?'" (Lk 12: 16 – 20). This man just heard one word from the Lord "FOOL"!

Solomon, the Wise king says, "To everything there is a season, a time for every purpose under heaven" (Ecc 3:1). So what is the time set for repentance?! Of course it is not in your old age!! An elder once said, "Repentance is a mother. Look after the mother so she can give you lovely children." The "children" symbolise the virtues which arise from repentance.

BEWARE OF LOSING HOPE:

Satan might try to let you lose hope, but look at your master and remember His great love towards sinners. Do not be afraid, "For you did not receive the spirit of bondage again to fear, but you received the Spirit of adoption by whom we cry out, "Abba, Father." (Rom 8: 15). Ask the Lord and He will grant you repentance and forgiveness, "Restore me, and I will return, For You are the Lord my God." (Jer 31:18)

The most acceptable prayer to the Lord is that of the repentant because by it, we are fulfilling the will of God, "For this is good and acceptable in the sight of God our Saviour, Who desires all men to be saved and to come to the knowledge of the truth." (1 Tim. 2:3-4)

Sometimes we ask for certain things and God doesn't fulfil them because as a Loving Father, He knows that they are not beneficial for our salvation. Even if I am asking for a virtue, He might see that gaining this virtue before the assigned time is not good for me, or maybe I am not spiritually ready for it. Thus the result would be vain glory and pride, and of course this is against God's will!! But the prayer which is for my salvation will never be rejected by God. St Isaac says; "There is nothing more beloved to the Lord than a person asking for repentance and forgiveness for his sins. God immediately responds to this prayer."

Remembering our sins can sometimes make us lose hope, as this is a scheme launched by Satan. There is another kind of "losing hope" which attacks at the beginning of our path to repentance. That is, making the struggle look so hard, with lots of obstacles, weariness and boredom.

This makes the repentant give up from the beginning. However, always remember that the way to heaven is not an easy one, as the Lord Christ said, "Narrow is the gate and difficult is the way which leads to life," (Mt 7: 14)

Many go back to their old sins as soon as they start the path of repentance. The Lord had delivered the children of Israel from Egypt, with His Mighty arm, yet, as soon as they reached the wilderness, they wanted to return to the land of slavery because of its materialistic goodness. They preferred garlic and leeks as slaves, over freedom and the food of the angels in the wilderness.

A very important concept in the spiritual life is 'Forcing yourself.' This means not giving yourself up to whatever the flesh asks for; otherwise no one would fast, pray or struggle in any spiritual battlefield. The Lord Jesus Christ says, "And from the days of John the Baptist until now, the kingdom of heaven suffers violence, and the violent take it by force." (Mt 11: 12). St. Paul emphasised this by saying, "You have not yet resisted to bloodshed, striving against sin." (Heb 12: 4)

The more we push ourselves in our spiritual struggle, the more support we will receive from heaven.However, things are not always difficult in the path to heaven because the promises of God encourage us and His hidden comforts calm us down. His voice within our hearts sustains and strengthens us, and at one point in time, He will see our sincere struggles and ease our way.

St. Macarius the Great says: "Whatever you do forcing yourself, God will give it to you, one day without any effort."

ALL SINS COULD BE FORGIVEN:

No matter how horrible your sins, as long as you are sincere in your repentance, your sins will be forgiven. The Lord Jesus says, "Assuredly, I say to you, all sins will be forgiven the sons of men, and whatever blasphemies they may utter; but he who blasphemes against the Holy Spirit never has forgiveness, but is subject to eternal condemnation"— because they said, "He has an unclean spirit." (Mk 3: 28-30)

Blasphemy against the Holy Spirit is a spiritual state where a person continually resists and willingly refuses to listen to the rebuke of the Holy Spirit within himself. This blasphemy is not forgiven. It is not like other sins such as killing, adultery or stealing. Someone might commit the worst sin, or speak ignorantly about the Son of God, as was the case of St. Paul, but all can be forgiven through the work of the Holy Spirit within us. However, he who is stubborn and refuses the work of the Holy Spirit will not be forgiven, "And when He has come, He will convict the world of sin…." (Jn 16: 8)

St. Isaac of Syria says: "There is no sin without forgiveness except that without repentance."

BEWARE OF RELUCTANCY AND REMEMBER JUDGMENT DAY:

Beware of misunderstanding God's great mercies. Do not depend on His kindness by thinking that God never punishes, St. John Chrysostom says:

"If you do not believe in heavenly punishment, then tell me what was the cause of the flood during the days of Noah? What caused the destruction of Sodom and Gomorrah together with seven cities and all the homosexuals? Why was Pharaoh and his chariots drowned in the Red Sea? Who destroyed 600,000 Jews in the wilderness? Who burnt Abraham's tent? Who ordered the earth to swallow Korah, Dathan and Abraham alive? Who killed 70,000 people during the time of David the King? Who killed 85,000 Assyrians in one night?"

Beware of being complacent on God's mercy and acting ignorantly. Listen to the Lord Jesus addressing the Jews: "I tell you, no; but unless you repent you will all likewise perish." (Lk 13:5) We've mentioned before that we are at the age of mercy, hereafter will be the age of justice. There is a great difference in God's way of dealing with human beings in both situations!!

God was incarnated and offered us an everlasting salvation. He will come back to judge the living and the dead and give everyone according to his deeds. In His first coming, no one knew Him, yet he came as a Shepherd seeking after lost sheep. "And being found in appearance as a man, He humbled Himself and became obedient to the point of death, even the death of the cross." (Phil 2: 8) But in His Second Coming, He will come in His Glory and in His Father's Glory, surrounded by His saints and angels. He will not come in a manger. He will not be judged like sinners or crucified between two robbers, but He will be sitting on the Throne of Justice.

In His first coming, "He will not cry out, or raise his voice in the streets. A bruised reed he will not break, and smoking flax He will not quench" (Isa 42: 2-3). In His Second Coming, He will come with the sound of thunder, trumpets, falling stars and shakes of the heaven. All elements will melt with fervent heat.

In His first coming, He was long-suffering, having patience with the sinners, as He said to the adultrous woman, "neither do I condemn you." (Jn 8: 11) He tolerated those who insulted Him and He forgave them. However, in His Second Coming, He will be a just judge giving everyone according to his deeds.

In His first coming He came as a groom, saying to every single soul, "Listen, O daughter, consider and incline your ear; Forget your own people also, and your father's house; So the King will greatly desire your beauty; because He is your Lord, worship Him." (Ps 45:10-11). He resembled the human soul to a virgin waiting for her bridegroom and He offered a precious dear dowry; His Blood.

In His Second Coming, He will come as an invading King to judge the rebellious to whom He had sent many prophets and ambassadors, yet they never listened and they went ahead killing and destroying.

This is the Day of Judgment, "for the hour is coming in which all who are in the graves will hear His voice and come forth—those who have done good, to the resurrection of life, and those who have done evil, to the resurrection of condemnation" (Jn 5: 28-29).

On that day, the sinners will not know what to do, "And the kings of the earth, the great men, the rich men, the commanders, the mighty men, every slave and every free man, hid themselves in the caves and in the rocks of the mountains, and said to the mountains and rocks, "Fall on us and hide us from the face of Him who sits on the throne and from the wrath of the Lamb! For the great day of His wrath has come, and who is able to stand?" (Rev 6: 15-17)

However, we should thank God who is patient with us and gives us a chance to bear fruits worthy of repentance. In kindness, He lifted up the axe from the root of the tree and left it for another year. Let's make use of the time for the days are evil. Let's wake up before it's too late!

CHARACTERISTICS OF A REPENTANT PERSON

The life of repentance is very special as it has its own characteristics and virtues and it brings forth a clear and repentant heart. The stronger and more sincere the repentance is, the more clearly these Characteristics appear in one's life and attitude:

A CONTRITE SOUL:

A repentant person is someone who rises up from sin and rises above any feeling of past humiliation. All his sins, iniquities and faults are before his eyes, and because of this shame, he has a contrite soul before the Lord.

Contrition of the soul and remembrance of sins are companions in the life of repentance. We will gain contrition of the soul if we place our sins and iniquities before our eyes at all times. People with sensitive natures will see the seriousness of their sins and feel more remorse. Thus, they offer more repentance. Blessed is the repentant person who sits daily with himself, remembers his sins and blames himself, crying before the Lord. Blessed is the person who remembers his iniquities if praised by people. The repentant person increases in grace, always looking deep within himself and opening up with the Lord.

St. Paul the Apostle kept remembering his sins, although he did it out of ignorance and holy zeal as he says, "For I am the least of the apostles, who am not worthy to be called an apostle, because I persecuted the church of God." (1 Cor 15: 9). Remember that St Paul was taken to the third heaven and saw unutterable things.

TEARS:

A repentant person becomes very sensitive when he remembers his own sins as well as the sins of others. He stands before God in tears while doing metanias and reciting the Psalms. Sometimes people repent while talking to others. David the Prophet was repenting in his sleep (Psalm 6) and while eating (Psalm 102).

These are the tears of sensitivity, not of fear; tears of someone who feels he has humiliated His beloved, although the sin is forgiven. A sensitive soul can't imagine it had committed such sins, it is regretful all the time, and thus cries.

After an action is done, it is too late to rewind. The only thing possible is to apologise, regret and offer repentance.

The saints shed many tears which we read about in their biographies; Tears of love, joy, sharing and repentance. St Bebnouda narrated about himself, "When I was a lad, I found a cucumber on the ground which had fallen from someone. I took it and ate it. Whenever I remember this incident, I weep." Later, he became a monk, grew in virtues, performed miracles and followed in the steps of St. Macarius, yet, whenever he remembered this incident, he wept....

TAKING THE LAST SEAT:

A person who is contrite in the inside is also contrite in the outside because his inner emotions overflow to his outer dealings. From inside, he feels he is a sinner and the least deserving. As a result, he never condemns others because he knows how heavy his sins are. He is always taking the last seat among others; assured that if people find out about his sins, they will rather cast him out.

So if he is invited to a spiritual meeting or a celebration, he goes while feeling unworthy to sit amongst those saints. He takes the last seat, thinking to himself, Is Saul also among the prophets? He has the same attitude when going to church or attending any gathering. He never talks a lot but always listens.

In his natural behaviour, he gives honour to others, not himself. He respects everyone; young and old. People might call him humble because he feels his unworthiness. He does not act this way to attract people's praise. Even if people ignore him, he never focuses on it or gets disturbed. He gains the virtue of tolerance because he considers any hardship, a result of his unworthiness.

HUMILITY:

It is a natural virtue of a contrite person who is always blaming himself. He never boasts, talks with authority or praises himself. He never mentions any of his good deeds but mentions his faults and falls. He doesn't accept praise from others and never defends himself.

CAUTIOUS:

A repentant person who has tried sin and experienced its pressure and severity is always cautious in his behaviour. He is aware of his weakness and so fears any other fall. He takes care of trifle things lest they should stumble him. As a result, he flees from any cause of sin. This high level of awareness prevented famous repentant saints from going back to their old sins.

PRACTICING ALL THE VIRTUES WITH THE SPIRIT OF REPENTANCE:

Virtues of repentance are very unique as they are characterised with humility and unworthiness. Everyone fasts, but a repentant person fasts in a special manner. He feels that he is not worthy to enjoy food or luxurious items. For example, there is a story written in 'The Paradise of Monks' about a soldier who offered repentance and was living an ascetic life. When people found out about him, they started coming and honouring him. He left that place telling himself; "Let's go where we are fed with the food of animals since we have done the deeds of animals!"

Questions & Answers

Q.1 Does repentance have different stages?

Some repentant saints, such as St. Augustine and St Moses the Black, repented in a sudden way because of their willing hearts and support by the Lord's grace. However repentance has many stages…

• The first stage involves identifying and repenting the sin.

• This is followed by a "struggle with the sin" as the devil will not cease to fight the repentant. The devil will remind the repentant of previous sins committed and will set traps of despair and guilt. The repentant person should be aware of all these tricks. St. Paul says, "For the flesh desires what is contrary to the Spirit, and the Spirit what is contrary to the flesh. They are in conflict with each other, so that you are not to do whatever you want." (Gal 5: 17)

• The third stage is overcoming the sin mentally. That is, being convinced that sin is a wrong doing and leads to negative consequences. This is itself a victory.

• Next, there is the struggle of removing the sin from the heart; where all bad desires lie. At this stage, the repentant needs to follow certain spiritual practices under the guidance of a spiritual guide.

• Full repentance is the stage where a person totally hates and repulses sin. This is described by St. Paul "be haters of evil."

Q. 2 LIFE WITH GOD IS A JOYFUL ONE, WHILE LIFE OF REPENTANCE IS ONE OF REGRET AND GRIEF. HOW CAN A REPENTANT COMBINE BOTH?

There is no contradiction between joy and grief in a repentant heart. He grieves in hope and at the same time rejoices for coming back to God. Hope is a great Christian virtue; like faith and love (1 Cor 13:13). Grief and the regret of previous sins should be mingled with hope. This leads to peace, joy and calmness.

A repentant person grieves because he has humiliated God; exchanging the Lord's Great Love with ingratitude and rebellion. Yet, at the same time, the repentant remembers God's promises and his call for all sinners. All these wonderful thoughts cast fear out of his heart because "there is no fear in love" (1 Jn 4:18)

After the repentant has returned to God, joy overflows in his heart. He feels God working in his heart and feels the Holy Spirit enlightening his path.

EXAMPLES OF REPENTANT PEOPLE

DAVID THE PROPHET: (2 SAM. 11: 12)

When King David saw a lady bathing, he couldn't resist sin and committed two horrible faults: adultery and murder. However, the wonderful mercies of the Lord interfered, sending Nathan the Prophet to rebuke King David, leading to his repentance in humbleness and regret. The Lord accepted his repentance as Nathan says, "The Lord also has put away your sin; you shall not die." (2 Sam 12: 13) Nonetheless, David still regretted his sin and cried a lot saying "My sin is always before me."

ST. MOSES THE BLACK (4TH CENTURY):

At the start of his life, he was the head of a gang, killing and robbing people. At the end of his life, he was a great ascetic saint and a guide to thousands of saints and seekers of the Lord.

The kind beloved Lord desired to reveal Himself to Moses. While he was heading towards the wilderness of Scetis, probably escaping some guards, he met an elder monk. After listening to the monk, his heart softened to repentance and he decided to stay in the wilderness. He confessed his sins to St. Isidorous and started his severe struggle and asceticism, making up for all the evil things he had done in the past. He later became a spiritual father for many and a renowned teacher in the wilderness. His body is still lying in the wilderness of Scetis, next to the body of his spiritual guide.

St. Augustine (354-430 AC)

One of the greatest authors, philosophers and teachers in the Eastern and Western Churches is St Augustine. He is a bishop and saint whose repentance and holiness exceeded his previous sins and iniquities.

His mother was a very pious Christian who taught him the basics of Christianity and spirituality, yet he forgot all of it after finishing his studies with pagan teachers. He kept reading books of pagan philosophers and poets, and then deviated and indulged in adultery. After his repentance, he wrote, "I used to get ashamed of not committing adultery, with no modesty whatsoever." His pious mother never gave up on him but followed him from one place to another, shedding tears about which St. Ambrose said, "Be sure that the son of those tears will never perish."

He came back to the Lord at the age of 33, offering sincere repentance and tears. He sold all his possessions and gave the money to the poor, before becoming a monk and starting a life of prayers, asceticism, teaching, publishing and service. He was ordained priest and later a bishop for a city in North Africa. He became one of the greatest and most famous Christian philosophers and interpreters of the Holy Bible. He defended the faith and argued with heretics. His most famous book is 'The Confessions' which he started by writing: "O God, You created us for You, our hearts will never find rest except in You."

ST. BAEISA:

St Baeisa was born in Menouf (Egypt) to wealthy parents and grew up in a pious atmosphere. When her parents departed, she turned her house into a resort for strangers and the needy, spending all her wealth to serve them. Some evil people attracted her to sin and her house became a brothel. The elders of Scetis heard about what happened and they grieved a lot. They delegated St. John the Short to go and drag her out of this perishable life. As soon as he saw her, he said, "Why did you belittle Lord Jesus and commit this iniquity?" St John then knelt down and started weeping, and St Baeisa was terrified. St John told her, "I can see the devils dancing before your face!" She asked him, "Is there is any chance for me to repent?" When he answered positively, she left her house and started walking with him in the wilderness.

At night, he asked her to lie down till morning while he stood afar off to pray. He then saw a pillar of light coming down from heaven and the angels of God carrying her spirit. When he came closer, he found her dead. He wept bitterly and prayed fervently asking the Lord to reveal to him her fate as he feared she didn't have enough time to repent. Immediately, he heard a voice from heaven saying: "Her repentance was accepted the minute she prayed. Her repentance was more sincere than others who spend years offering repentance."

ST. MARY THE EGYPTIAN: (FIRST HALF OF THE FIFTH CENTURY)

She left her parents' house and headed to Alexandria at the age of 12, where she spent 17 years living a lustful life and stumbling lots of youth. One day she boarded a ship going to Jerusalem to celebrate the Feast of the Cross. In Jerusalem, she tried to enter the church like everyone else, to receive the blessings of the wood of the Holy Cross. Yet she felt a hidden hand preventing her. After many attempts, she still couldn't enter the church. She started meditating on her defiled life and looked to the icon of St. Mary. She prayed fervently and vowed to repent and spend the rest of her life in the wilderness if God allowed her to enter the Church. She then was able to enter the church.

She departed to another church where she had confession and partook of the Holy Communion. She headed to the wilderness of Jordan at the age of 29. This repentant saint lived there for 47 years leading a life of harsh asceticism and holiness. The devil constantly fought her by reminding her of her previous lustful life. She became a hermit and the Lord granted her the gift of prophecy and disclosing the unknown. During this period, she never saw a human being, except St. Zosima the priest, who gave her Holy Communion before her departure and wrote her biography.

DEACON HABIB FARAG: (1941)

We've known this person closely. He used to be a servant in Sunday School. He started a licentious life away from God but he departed in peace as a pure pious soul. He even knew the time of his departure and wrote it in his diary!!

At the beginning, he always refused to go to church or attend any meetings at St. Anthony's Church in Shoubra,

Cairo, regardless of how his friends tried to attract him. Finally, he agreed to attend a meeting on a condition that no one asks him to come again, and that no one visits him at home concerning this issue.

At church, he was greatly touched with what he heard, and at night he saw a vision; St. Mary took him to Hades where he saw people crying and moaning. He asked her to take him out of this horrible place. St. Mary then took him to Paradise, where he saw the luminous saints and fathers and she started introducing them; Abraham, David the Prophet, St. Anthony…etc. He saw them sitting on chairs of light but there was an empty chair. When he asked about it, St. Mary answered, "This is your chair if you follow Jesus Christ!"

When he woke up, he was yearning more and more for the chair that was waiting for him. He started to live a life of repentance and harsh spiritual struggle. The Lord revealed His glory through his pious righteous life. Sometimes when he prayed in his bedroom, he saw light surrounding him and his stretched hands looked like lit candles. He departed in peace at the age of 27.

WHAT THE FATHERS SAID ABOUT REPENTANCE

ST EPHRAIM THE SYRIAN:

"Fill your eyes with tears and the eyes of your mind will soon be opened. Come together, rich and poor, princes and subjects, young men and maidens, old men and children, every age and gender, who desire to be delivered from eternal torments and to inherit the Kingdom of Heaven. With holy David, let us beseech our merciful and most gracious Lord, saying, "Open Thou mine eyes, that I may see the wondrous things of Thy law. Enlighten my eyes, lest I sleep the sleep of death." Let us cry as the blind man who sat by the wayside saying, "Thou Son of the Most High God, have mercy upon me!" And if any rebuke us, or charge us to hold our peace, let us cry the more, a great deal, and never be weary of crying, till Christ, the giver of lights, opens the eyes of our hearts. Therefore draw near to Him and be enlightened, and your faces shall not be ashamed."

He encourages repentance by saying, "My Brothers, let us repent and bring forth fruits worthy of repentance while we still have time. Hear what Our Lord says, 'There shall be joy in heaven over one sinner that repents!' Why then, O sinner, do you act negligent, sitting there aimlessly? Why are you disheartened and in despair? If there will be joy in heaven at your repentance, what are you afraid of? The angels are so affected as to feel an extraordinary joy on your account, and how can you remain inactive, unconcerned and unmoved? The King of Angels preaches repentance. Are there any fears which discourage you? The Holy Undivided Trinity, whom we worship, invites you to repentance. Are you going to return to him a fruitless sigh and groan?"

He talks about the importance of repentance especially on Judgment day: "Does it strike no terror into you, which in that hour everyone shall receive in proportion to his merits, according to his works done in the body? Every man shall bear his own burden, and everyone shall reap whatsoever he has sown here. All must stand naked and undisguised before the Judgment Seat of Christ and every one of us must give an account of himself to the Judge. In that time and place, none can possibly receive any benefit or assistance from anyone else. One brother or friend shall not be able to help another, nor parents their children, nor children their parents, nor husbands their wives, but everyone shall stand with fear and trembling, awaiting the sentence which shall be pronounced by God.

Why don't we get ready while we still have the chance? Why do we belittle the Holy Books and the words of Christ? Do you think that His sayings and His saints will not condemn you on that day if you are reluctant in following them? The Lord Jesus told His disciples, "He who hears from you, hears from Me and he who disobeys you, disobeys Me." In another part He says, "He who disobeys Me and ignores my words, I will not condemn him, but the sayings which I have said will condemn him."

Blessed are those who hunger and thirst for they will

be filled but woe to those who were filled for they will be hungry and thirsty hereafter. Blessed are those who wept, for they will laugh and be comforted hereafter, but woe to those who are laughing now for they will cry and weep hereafter. Blessed are those who were merciful on earth for they shall receive mercy hereafter, but woe to the merciless...

The Lord Jesus reminds us: "I did not come to call the righteous, but sinners to repentance", also, "those who are well have no need of a physician, but those who are sick."

If the Lord Himself is saying these words, why are you reluctant? Come to the Lord with all your wounds, evils and iniquities. He is a Merciful and Kind Physician. He was incarnated for your sake!! You never know when He will close the door, after which there is no room for repentance!!

SAINT JOHN SABA: (THE SPIRITUAL ELDER)

"O great mercy, how abundant you are. Who does not marvel at your mercy O Lord? And who does not confess to Your grace? You have granted us a new mother by the new birth. We have lived in evil and wickedness, but repentance can purify us and enlighten us. Adam had children from Eve; they resembled the physical world. Likewise, Jesus, from baptism and repentance, bears children who resemble Him for the spiritual world. He says to us, 'Repent, for the kingdom of heaven is at hand.' Our Father, show us repentance. It is in the narrow gate; whoever endures its darkness and difficulties, will enjoy the kingdom of light. This gate of repentance is inside you;

the entrance to the true life."

Repentance is the mother of life. Blessed is the one who is born of it, for he will never die. Christ calls everyone to repent but the devil prevents people from hearing that calling and he covers their heart with his trickery and cleverness. Repentance is the toxin that saves from the fatal pangs of sin and is a great torment to the adversary. It saves and liberates the slaves who were enslaved by Satan's wickedness. It wastes the efforts of Satan in just one hour.

Repentance changes adulterers into celibates. It is the fire which burns the weed and the water which irrigates the holy plants. It is the intercessor of the captives. Who does not love you, O repentance, who carries all the blessings? Only the devil hates you for you have taken away his wealth, properties and made him empty from his inheritance that he once plundered. No one ascended to heaven without you. No one with you, goes to Hades. Who can see God without repentance? Who abided in you with hope and fell into Satan's hand? Who was purified without being washed by you? Who watered his plants from your rain and did not reap the fruits of joy? Who did not wipe his face with the tears of repentance and did not see God in his heart? Who took you as an intercessor, and did not enter into the door of divine treasures? You saved David from sin and you saved the people of Nineveh. Blessed are you, O mother of forgiveness, whom God has granted to be the intercessor of sinners. God will never close His door if you ask Him, for He has given you the keys of the kingdom."

A PRAYER OF REPENTACE BY: ST. SHENOUDA THE ARCHIMANDRITE

O Lord, forgive me the sinner. I can't even lift my eyes to you as I am ashamed of the multitude of my sins. O Lord, do not count my iniquities but rather deal with me according to the multitude of Your mercies. O Lord, I plead and ask You for my miserable soul and body. Let me do Your will and let Your mercy guide me. My Lord, forgive my sins, heed my iniquities and save me from Your anger and wrath. What will I say when I stand before You? Protect me from the traps of the devil. Grant me Your peace and the blessings of Your Holy Name. O Lord, dwelling in heaven, have mercy on me. Do not let me fall in the hands of the enemy. I depend on You, O Christ Son of God. If I lean towards sin, do not abandon me. Do not allow me to follow my lustful desires.

Do not allow me to be blamed on Judgment Day. Do not judge me according to my sins. Clothe me before Your Fearful Chair. Cleanse me so that I stand pure before Your Hands. O Lover of Mankind, shield my soul with Your Pure Blood.

O Lord, control my desire of sin. Awake me from my slumber, preserve me from deviation and always keep Your Name on my lips. Let Your pure angel cast away all the blasphemy of sin. Make me worthy of the dwelling of Your Holy Spirit. Let my soul and spirit praise You all the days of my life. Please Lord, hear my prayers according to Your mercy. Accept my pleadings, save me so that I do not sin and guide me to do Your will. Do not deprive me of Your grace. Purify my heart, tongue and all my senses. Take off my stony heart and grant me a contrite heart to plead before you. Do not reject me because You have invited me. I am idolatrous because of my sins. Have mercy on me for You have the authority of mercy. Make me worthy to bless You till the last breath. Abide Your holy words in my heart and soul. Save me from the traps of the devil. Have mercy on me and hear my cry. Let my prayers stand before You as a sweet incense aroma between Your hands. Do not judge your servant because no one is justified before You. Glory, honour and dominion to You forever. Amen.

Confession

𝓧

"If we confess our sins, He is faithful and just to forgive us our sins and to cleanse us from all unrighteousness"
(1Jn 1:9)

❧ The Importance of Confession and its Blessings

❧ The Three Elements of Confession

❧ General Guidelines

❧ Self Examination before Confession

❧ Prayers Before and After Confession

THE IMPORTANCE OF
CONFESSION AND ITS BLESSINGS

The Mystery of Confession has many important blessings in chastising the soul and building our spiritual life. Ever since the early Apostolic era (Acts 19: 18), our holy church assures the importance of having confession regularly and honestly. In addition to the verses and verifications of the Holy Bible, the importance of confession is also mentioned in the writings of early church fathers such as Dionysius the Areopagite, Clement of Rome, Irenaeus of Lyons (the Apostles' disciple), Athanasius the Apostolic, Basil the Great, John Chrysostom, Tertullian, and Origen.

In the early ages when life was more simple and less complicated than our era, the church used to practice the Mystery of Confession strictly and regularly. How much more important is confession nowadays with such a busy life style? We can all feel the many benefits of confession and its deep impact psychologically, spiritually, socially and even physically.

Psychologically:

It is a natural instinct for a human being to feel the need to disclose what's troubling him/her and confess his/her sins. After confessing, the person is relieved. Our conscience tells us to get rid of our sins and iniquities through confession, after which, we become calmer and peaceful. We can also seek guidance from our Confession Father regarding complex problems and situations, otherwise the problems continue to escalate. With these escalated problems, an individual might isolate himself from society and feel psychologically burdened. However, people who are internally happy can mingle comfortably with others and never lose their inner peace.

<u>Spiritually:</u>

Through confession, we gain something that nothing in this world can provide that is Jesus Christ, who is the Redeemer and Forgiver of our many sins. Through Him we gain eternal life in heaven, which is more precious than anything in this vain world.

Through confession, we are able to partake of His Holy Body and Precious Blood which makes us worthy of abiding in Jesus; "He who eats My flesh and drinks My blood abides in Me, and I in him." (Jn 6: 56) Without confession, we do not deserve the grace of partaking in Holy Communion, "For he who eats and drinks in an unworthy manner eats and drinks judgment to himself, not discerning the Lord's body." (1 Cor 11:29)

Another benefit of confession is that by disclosing our thoughts to our confession father, we can dismiss and get rid of them. Nothing makes the devils rejoice more than when we conceal our thoughts because they can then strengthen their fight against us as we stand alone in the battlefield. Solomon the wise writes, "But woe to him who is alone when he falls, for he has no one to help him up."

(Eccles 4: 10).

St. John Cassian says: "He who discloses his thoughts to his spiritual guide can never be deceived." He also says, "Sin abides if we heed it in our hearts, but as soon as we confess our sins it is gone even before the confession father says anything. Just like when you lift up a rock that a snake is hiding under and it runs away. Satan is the old snake. When you reveal him and expose him to the light, he flees away as he is the father of darkness and could never stand the light. Also Satan is haughty so as soon as you reveal his deceit, he gets infuriated and escapes because of his pride."

It is mentioned about St. Macarius the Great that while walking in the wilderness, he met Satan and asked him how things were going with the monks. Satan answered: "very bad and miserable, because the monks disclose to their guides every evil and deceitful thought which I try to implant in their minds, except just one monk (name) who is my best friend as I can mislead him however I like." The saint headed straightaway to the cell of that monk and advised him not to conceal any evil thought but rather open up with his spiritual father; the monk accepted his advice and obeyed. After a while St. Macarius met Satan again, but this time Satan was so furious and kept saying that this monk was not his friend anymore!!

Through confession, God gives us solutions to our problems and remedies to our weaknesses. It is said that one of the Egyptian monks fasted for a long time asking the Lord for a solution for a certain problem. When he didn't get a solution, he decided to go and ask the elders. As soon as he came out of his cell, an angel prevented him from going further and gave him the answer to his problem saying: "you deserved an answer for your problem because of your humility and your decision to go and ask the elders; more than the period for which you had fasted."

This is clarified in the Holy Bible, "Now it happened as He went to Jerusalem that He passed through the midst of Samaria and Galilee. Then as He entered a certain village, there met Him ten men who were lepers, who stood afar off. And they lifted up their voices and said, "Jesus, Master, have mercy on us!" So when He saw them, He said to them, "Go, show yourselves to the priests." And so it was that as they went, they were cleansed." (Lk 17:11-14). Jesus told them to go and show themselves to the priests and on their way they were healed. We can see that it pleases the Lord when we subdue to people whom He has given the authority to act on behalf of others. This is also clear through the great works He performs through them.

The spiritual discipleship is another great benefit of confession. Our Lord Jesus Christ's last message to His disciples was, "Go therefore and make disciples of all the nations, baptizing them in the name of the Father and of the Son and of the Holy Spirit, teaching them to observe all things that I have commanded you; and lo, I am with you always, even to the end of the age." Amen. (Mt 28: 19-20). He paved this path for us practically by appointing disciples and handling them His commandments for us to fulfil. Life of discipleship has numerous benefits, for spiritual virtues are not only acquired through reading books or listening to lectures, but also through spiritual teachers, similar to an apprentice getting trained by an expert.

Socially:

Confession provides a person with a healthy understanding of the person and his relationship with others, thus helping the individual in his healing process from any psychological imbalance caused by the guilt of sin. Therefore, confession, a person is able to interact in the society in a healthy manner.

4. Physically:

We learn from the Holy Bible that sin was the reason for some diseases, as was the case of the man healed by the Pool of Bethesda (Jn 5:15). As a consequence, our church encourages confession before the Mystery of the Unction of the Sick. Modern science also confirms this as the body is affected by problems and psychological shocks. This is a new branch of science called 'Psycho Somatic Medicine'.

Thus, confession heals the body and the spirit. It releases those who are bound to bad habits, those who are chocked with psychological complexes, those who are slaves to certain illusions, those who have deviated from the normal way of life and those who cannot live in harmony with society around them. In one phrase, confession releases a person from the bitter consequences of sin.

The Mystery of Confession has been practiced by our church for the past eighteen centuries. Its knowledge was not a result of research and studies, but was the result of fulfilling the commandments of our Lord Jesus Christ who created man and understands all about the inner self.

In addition to the spiritual experience of the church, it is supported by the hidden work of God and the spirituality of this great Mystery of confession.

Confession is not just a psychological treatment; otherwise it would resemble the jobs of psychologists who treat people psychologically, while they themselves might be non-believers. However confession is a great Church Mystery which includes many benefits. This Mystery is accompanied by the forgiveness of sins through the absolution prayed by the confession father; something which no clinic in the world can offer, no matter how experienced and educated they are.

Duty of the Church:

Our church traditions assure that not every priest can be a confession father except those who meet the requirements of leading and guiding others. The bishop used to give this entitlement to a priest after he was sure that the priest is capable. It is not necessary that every priest should be a confession father. Although age is an important element concerning experience and spiritual knowledge, the priest must also have wise spiritual discernment in order to listen to confessions.

St. Isaiah (4th century) advised the novices saying: "If an elder asked you about your thoughts, disclose them frankly as long as you are sure he is honest and keeps your confession. Do not only consider his old age, but also depend on his knowledge, experience and spiritual awareness, lest he should add to your misery instead of offer healing."

St. John Cassian (4th century) said: "Anba Moses commands us not to conceal our thoughts, but rather disclose them to spiritual elders who have knowledge and discernment. Many had disclosed their thoughts to elders, but as the latters lacked knowledge, they casted them in despair rather than provided remedy."

It is about time for the church to take this Mystery seriously. Theological courses should be prepared for priests and deacons, to enrich their knowledge and spiritual experiences regarding this Mystery. In cities such as Cairo and Alexandria, the church has established centres for confession where certain priests only serve the Mystery of Confession, not carrying out any other duty. In some churches, confession is conducted during the Holy Liturgy, leading to a loss of character and benefit.

THE THREE ELEMENTS OF CONFESSION

FIRST WITH MYSELF:

Necessity of Repentance:

We've mentioned previously that confession is the first practical step of repentance, which means that repentance from the depth of the heart should precede and accompany confession. Confession without repentance does not make sense, because the Mystery of Confession is also called the Mystery of Repentance. Confession is not just words said to the confession father, even if these words are true. The main foundation is a repentant heart.

Some people approach the priest before Holy Communion asking for absolution. If the priest asks them if they are ready for Holy Communion, they answer 'Thank God, there is nothing wrong' or 'we had Communion last week or three days ago' as if they lived three days without making a single mistake!!

St. Cyprian (3rd century) reproaches those who have Holy Communion without honest repentance by saying: "How can they have Holy Communion without repentance and confession, without having absolution from the priest or the bishop?" (Letter No. 9 part 2). Some people might have Communion regularly but not have confession daily; however we are not addressing these kinds of people. We are addressing those who do not care about confession totally.

Those who say 'Thank God there is nothing wrong' are misleading themselves. They are either hiding their sins and lying to the Truth, or unfortunately are not aware of themselves and are lying to God. St. John says: "If we say that we have no sin, we deceive ourselves, and the truth is not in us. If we confess our sins, He is faithful and just to forgive us our sins and to cleanse us from all unrighteousness. If we say that we have not sinned, we make Him a liar, and His word is not in us. (1 Jn 1: 8-10) Either way, these people do not benefit by any means from the absolution prayed by the priest if they do not confess.

It is a horrible sin as they belittle the Great Mystery. It adds to the confessor another sin in addition to the great sin of having Communion without confession!! Absolution without repentance and confession will never grant us forgiveness of sins. If this is not the case, confession would have vanished gradually, and forgiveness would have become something easy and trifle, being acquired without toil or effort. For example, an irresponsbile person who never knew God and never passed through the narrow gate of repentance would just come and receive absolution. This is not the teaching of Christianity.

Many people are proud of their sins, without any shame; however, we have to confess our sins in disgrace, humblenss and repentance because when God sees our heartfelt repentance, He forgives us. "For out of the abundance of the heart the mouth speaks." (Mt 12: 34) After building the House of God, Solomon the King said in his prayer to the Lord, "hear from heaven Your dwelling place, and forgive, and give to everyone according to all his ways, whose heart You know for You alone know the hearts of the sons of men" (2 Chr 6: 30).

Repentance is a main corner in the Mystery of Confession. A confessor should have the feeling that he has sinned before God who loves him. That is why he is coming with a contrite soul to apologise for his iniquities, deciding to abandon them forever, and ask for God's help and strength. David the Prophet says, "For I will declare my iniquity; I will be in anguish over my sin. (Ps 38: 18) Also, "A voice was heard on the desolate heights, weeping and supplications of the children of Israel. For they have perverted their way; They have forgotten the Lord their God" (Jer 3:21).

A Self Account:

Proper confession accompanied with repentance and regret needs preparation; which is called self account. Be strict and accurate with yourself. Compare God's kind and good dealings with your denial and harshness towards Him. Compare your life with the lifes of saints. Remember St. Peter's words, "If the righteous one is scarcely saved, where will the ungodly and the sinner appear?" (1 Pet 4: 18). Always remind yourself that you are a sinner. All of these feelings will give you the spirit of contrition and you will feel the deep need for God's grace.

This is the case if you are aware of your sins but sometimes we forget our sins; either because we do not give a proper self account and neglect confession for long periods of time or because we are so reluctant with our spiritual life that we lose our spiritual sensitivity, thus we sin without feeling it.

In this case, we have to pray a lot so that the Lord might clarify our sins. Plead to the Holy Spirit to help you and enlighten you with His Grace, saying with St. Augustine: "My God, let me know who You are and who am I." Our God is merciful and if you ask Him, He will grant you to remember your sins and acknowledge them. St Ephrem said about the Lord: "He is thirsty for the tears of a repentant person."

If you suffer from forgetting incidents, write them down regularly so you do not forget them during confession. For more privacy, you can just write symbols to remind yourself, as you are not writing details but just reminders. After confession, tear up this paper as your sins have been wiped away.

Talk to God:

When you feel the burden of your sins and you suffer from low self-esteem, close the door of your room and talk to Jesus. Spend your night in prayers, pleadings and tears, offering repentance. Have a proper detailed confession. God knows about your sins before you have committed them, but in confession you are announcing your iniquity and feeling guilty. David the Prophet said: "When I kept silent, my bones grew old through my groaning all the day long. For day and night Your hand was heavy upon me; My vitality was turned into the drought of summer. I acknowledged my sin to You and my iniquity I have not hidden. I said, "I will confess my transgressions to the Lord;" And You forgave the iniquity of my sin." (Ps 32: 3-5).

In your prayer to God, talk about yourself in detail, do not just talk in plural form. This will give you a deep feeling of guilt, instead of blaming others for your sins. So, when you pray for forgiveness, you do not say; "Forgive us O Lord and remit our sins, You know O Lord that we are weak" but rather say: "Forgive me My Lord and remit my sins, You know I am a weak sinner and frequently fall." How sweet and acceptable before God is the second statement. It also offers plenty of comfort and peace to the heart who prays it!

SECOND: BEFORE THE PRIEST:

Shyness:

One of the main things which delay confession is our shyness to disclose sins before the priest, but we have to overcome this feeling as it is beneficial for our spiritual life. If you were not shy of God when you committed sin, you shouldn't be shy before His delegate during confession. Although shyness is hard and troubling, it is good for you. It makes you feel the grievousness of sin and the bitterness of falling into it. That is why our early fathers said that the Mystery of Confession is a strong bridle which controls a person and prevents him from going back to sin. Joshua son of Sirach says: "do not be ashamed to confess your sins." (Sirach 4: 26)

Sometimes out of ignorance, a person falls into some sins which are very shameful to talk about before the priest. But you have to remember that the priest is listening to many sins from different people and you are not the first. He is used to all kinds of sin and he is always expecting to hear unpleasant and impure matters.

Shyness may lead some people into having confession directly with God instead of the priest. In this case, pride is added to shyness, because a proud person always wants to look pious and saintly before people.

This is a famous Satanic trick which prevents people from the blessings gained through confession. Let's put aside all of these issues, and think of the blessings and peace of confession. For there is no one without sin on earth even if he is to live one day!!

How to confess:

1. Beware of over familiarity with your confession father. Always remember that you are about to perform a great Mystery, renewing your life in a rebirth. Forget all about your personal relationship with him and think about him as a delegate from God. Talk about your sins in awe and pain, not as someone retelling stories.

2. Confess all your sins: those which you did, said, thought or acted. You have to know that any unconfessed sin will stay with you, no matter how well you are improving. It will keep bothering you even if you become a saint. Empty your heart of every sin. The holy inspired words of Jeremiah the Prophet addressing each soul: "I called for my lovers, but they deceived me; My priests and my elders breathed their last in the city, while they sought food to restore their life." (Lam 1:19). It is a very accurate metaphor, highlighting the importance of emptying our hearts during confession. If you empty a cup containing oil or honey, it will still carry some traces. If you empty a cup containing vinegar or wine, it will keep its smell. However, a cup of water will not leave any traces; exactly like a pure heart after confessing all the sins within.

3. Care about the details of your sin, no matter how

horrible it is. Be honest before your confession father. This includes the place of sin, time, and the person(s) you sinned against (you don't have to mention names). But you will not benefit well if you give a very brief summary of your sins. For example, your general confession may be: "My father, I am not praying properly, I don't like others according to God's commandments and I am having Communion with disrespect" Such a confession wouldn't let the father confessor know much about your state. All the saints could say these words because no matter how high their spiritual level, they will still feel a shortage in fulfilling the Lord's commandments. But talking specifically about your sins will help the priest in deciding on a proper remedy for your weakness. There is a big difference between saying; "Father I looked in an unclean way" and saying; "Father I looked in an unclean way while being at church," or saying: "I am fighting certain thoughts about this girl and feeling attracted to her" and saying; "I am living with this girl in the same house." The second is a serious case and needs special remedy.

Thus we can see that mentioning the details of our sins will clarify our habits, unclean thoughts and emotions, giving the priest a clear idea of how he can guide you to repentance.

4. Take care about the nature of sin: Is it a continuous sin or did it happen just once? Did it become a habit and is it hard to give up?

5. Care about your emotions while committing the sin: Were you enjoying it or were you disgusted?

6. Do not try to justify yourself during confession and blame others. Do not belittle your sin, i.e. you tell the priest that the devil had tricked you. Remember that any sin you commit is done out of your own free will. Don't blame others saying "Someone infuriated me and so I had to get angry at him." If he had truly infuriated you, where is the patience and love which tolerates all things?

7. Be honest in your confession and don't try to blame others because you are supposed to be ashamed of yourself. For example, someone might be asked about their religion and they might deny being Christian yet in confession, he confesses it as a sin of lying. There is a huge difference between denying faith and lying!!

8. Care about the positive side of your spiritual life in your confession; not only the negatives. As well as confessing your sins, talk about the virtues that you are lacking. St. James the Apostle says: "Therefore, to him who knows to do good and does not do it, to him it is sin." (Jas 4:17). As a Christian you have to grow spiritually, "till we all come to the unity of the faith and of the knowledge of the Son of God, to a perfect man, to the measure of the stature of the fullness of Christ;" (Eph 4:13). If you are not growing, it means there is still a sin fighting and preventing your growth. Examine yourself regarding Christian virtues, like love, duties of worship, self-denial, purity (of mind, body, senses and heart) and try to discover which virtues you are short of.

9. Don't think that your confession is only regarding spiritual issues; because the Lord Jesus orders us to be perfect; "Therefore you shall be perfect, just as your Father in heaven is perfect." (Mt 5:48) This includes perfectness

and honesty in everything. So a student who is not studying and wasting his time should confess this. Also an employee who is not performing his duties honestly.

10. Confess the sins which you already know a remedy for; don't hide sins even if you know how to deal with them, especially if you commit them frequently. The devil always fights people with such a thought, "You don't have to tell your confession father because he will tell you so and so and you know all about it so there is no need to confess it." We have to keep confessing those sins until we get rid of them. A person cannot be a good judge for himself. The waters of the rivers in Syria and Iraq were nicer and softer than the Jordan River, yet they were not good enough to heal Naaman the Syrian, compared to the waters of the Jordan River, which Elisha the Prophet recommended for his healing (2 Kings 5). God places power and grace in the words of our confession father for the benefit of the confessors who believe in the Mystery of Confession.

Confession is not only for healing, but for obtaining the absolution and blessing. There is no forgiveness without declaring your sins.

11. You have to open up with your confession father even if something is concerning him. If the devil stumbled you in any matter regarding your confession father, you have to mention it politely and ask him for clarification. For example, if he is always rushing you in confession, tell him that you do not feel comfortable this way.

12. Listen carefully to the advice of your confession father and accept it. If you do not feel content, tell him.

Informing your confession father with the remedies that work is just like a sick person who informs his doctor regarding the medicines that relieve him and those that do not.

THIRD: THE ABSOLUTION FROM SIN:

After confessing all your sins before the priest, kneel in awe and tell him; "Absolve me my father from the sins which I have confessed and also the hidden ones," as you might have forgotten some sins. The priest will then hold the cross over your head while praying the Absolution Prayer. This prayer includes pleadings and deep spiritual words. You will feel the strength of these words as they are prayed by the priest. The Absolution Prayer is divided into three parts:

THE FIRST ABSOLUTION:

"O Lord who has given us the authority to tread upon serpents and scorpions and upon all the power of the enemy, crush its head beneath our feet speedily. Scatter away every design of weakness that is against us, for You are the King of us all, O Christ our God".

THE SECOND ABSOLUTION:

"You, O Lord, created the heavens and You descended and became man for our salvation. You are He who sits upon the Cherubim and the Seraphim and beholds them who are lowly. You are He unto whom we lift up the eyes of our hearts. You are the Lord who forgives our iniquities and saves our souls from corruption. We worship Your unutterable compassion, and we ask You to give us Your peace, for You have given all things unto us.

Acquire us unto Yourself, God our Saviour, for we know none other but You; Your Holy Name we do utter. Turn us, O Lord, into fearing and desiring You. Be pleased that we abide in the enjoyment of Your good things. Those who have bowed their heads beneath Your hand, exalt them in their ways of life and adorn them with virtues. May we all be worthy of Your Kingdom in the heavens, through the goodwill of God, Your good Father."

THE THIRD ABSOLUTION:

"Master, Lord Jesus Christ, the only begotten Son and Logos of God the Father, Who has broken every bond of our sins through His saving, life-giving sufferings, who breathed into the face of His holy disciples and saintly Apostles, and said to them, "Receive the Holy Spirit. Whose sins you will remit, they are remitted to them, and those which you retain, they shall be retained." You also now, our Master, through Your holy apostles, have given grace to those who for a time labour in priesthood in Your Holy Church, to forgive sin upon the earth and to bind and to loose every bond of inquiry. Now, also, we ask and entreat Your goodness, O Lover of Mankind, for Your servants, my fathers, and my brethren and my weakness, those who bow their heads before Your Holy Glory. Dispense unto us Your mercy, and loose every bond of our sins, and if we have committed any sin against You, knowingly or unknowingly or through anguish of heart, or in deed, or in word, or from faint-heartedness, You O Master, who knows the weakness of men, as a good and loving God, grant us the forgiveness of our sins (the priest signs the confessing person, then says...) Bless us, purify us, absolve us (and absolve your servant ...). Fill us with Your fear, and straighten us unto Your holy, good will, for You are our God, and all glory, honour and dominion and adoration are due unto You."

The confessor feels he is not bowing his head before a human being but rather bowing under the Hand of God, as mentioned in the Second Absolution, "Your servant..... who is bending his head under Your Hand." The priest also announces that he is performing this Mystery according to a Divine authority by saying; "...You granted those serving in priesthood....to forgive sins....."

In the three Absolutions, the priest does not only plead for the confessor but also asks for his own weakness. He asks the Lord to grant the confessor many spiritual blessings like:

• Uprooting evil from our hearts and "Crushing its head beneath our feet speedily" because the head of anything is its beginning.

• To give us His peace which we have lost through sin.

• When the priest asks for peace he prays: "and we ask You to give us Your peace", and when he asks for God's fear he prays: "Turn us, God, into fearing You." St. Anthony says: "The beginning of wisdom is the fear of God, so if light comes into a dark house it will disperse the darkness. The same with the fear of God, if it enters the heart it will cast away ignorance and teach that person all virtues and wisdom."

• Our spiritual life tastes different as a result of sin. We start to lose our yearn for God. Similar to a sick person who tastes food differently because of his current illness. Thus the priest prays so that we may regain our love and desire for God, instead of being attracted to sin. "Draw me away, we will run after you" (Song of Songs 1:4)

RESULTS OF THE ABSOLUTION PRAYER:

• Remission of our sins; How we fell, whether knowingly or unknowingly.

• Remission of our sins; with its different kinds, whether by deeds or speech.

• Remission of our sins; as committed under different circumstances or out of faintheartedness.

• Gaining a blessing, purity and an unbinding of all the chains of sin and their authority.

• After the Absolution Prayer, be sure that the Lord has waived all your sins, remembering the prophet Nathan's words to King David, "So David said to Nathan, "I have sinned against the Lord." and Nathan said to David, "The Lord also has put away your sin; you shall not die." (2 Sam 12:13)

• In love and submission, we get to kiss the cross that the priest is holding.

GENERAL GUIDELINES

AFTER CONFESSION:

It is recommended that you go straight away and meditate on the Lord's mercies, making benefit of your spiritual state and storing what would be useful for the future. A very common mistake done by youth, is that they go confession in groups, spending the time before confession chatting and even exchanging jokes, as if they do not feel sorry for their sins. After confession, they remain with the same attitude, may be talking on their way back about issues which need another immediate confession!!

The confessor has to follow the priest's advices honestly and accurately. If a sick person does not use the prescribed medication, this will hurt him. Similarly, a confessor who does not carry out and follow the confession father's instructions will not benefit.

Do not fall into despair if you sin again after confession, but rise up and renew your vows with God, "For a righteous man may fall seven times and rise again," (Prov 24: 16). God knows our weak nature. He established the Mystery of Confession, so we can use over and over and thus come back to Him in regret every time we fall. The door of repentance is always open till the last breath of our lives. Blessed is the person who enters through it…

ONE CONFESSION FATHER:

The church teaches us to have only one confession father, unless we are travelling away or for any other specific reason. In this case, we have to have our confession father's permission to deal with another confession father. That is why you have to be very careful when choosing your spiritual physician. Beware of avoiding your confession father for an unholy reason or because you are failing in overcoming your sins. The church does not encourage those who move between confession fathers, and insists that they should have just one confession father for their spiritual advantage.

CHANGING CONFESSION FATHERS:

Sometimes the spiritual advices and guidelines offered by the confession father do not work with the confessor, and people might think is it alright to change confession fathers. Actually, as mentioned before, the confession father is like a physician, and a sick person might not find any benefit in dealing with the same doctor for a long period of time and so he changes. Sometimes the doctor himself suggests another doctor.

The utmost aim of confession is the spiritual welfare of the confessor, and so changing the confession father is alright. Sometimes some priests recommend specific priests for certain kinds of problems, as they might have a special gift in leading and comforting those confessors.

The confessor has to take permission from his confession father to change, out of courtesy and protocol, yet, it can be very hard to change.

Asking to change your confession father is not included in the priestly absolution, so if the confessor is sensitive, he can send a polite letter explaining the issue, asking his confession father for permission to change and to pray for him.

A question which always comes to our minds; in the case of changing the confession father, do I have to confess all my previous sins to which I already had an absolution?

The answer is no, because all the previous sins confessed are waived and there is no need to retell them again, except if the old sins have a relationship with the recent sins or for the sake of acknowledging the new confession father with your life style and problems.

FORGOTTON OR NEW SINS:

What happens if you forget to confess a specific sin then later remember it, or if you commit a sin after confession and before having Holy Communion?

Do not get disturbed; you can either tell it to one of the serving priest at that church, even if he is not your confession father, or you can have Holy Communion after the priest prays the absolution then confess it to your confession father when you meet him. This all depends on your confession father's instructions. It also depends on how you evaluate your sin. Yet it is preferable, if you are in doubt, not to partake of Holy Communion until you meet your confession father.

THE SPIRITUAL GUIDE:

You can have another spiritual guide other than your confession father. It could even be a layman, who guides you concerning general issues such as prayer, humility, pride, judging, etc. However, you should not go into details of your sins and your delicate private spiritual life. There are some things that only the confession father should know, because the spiritual guide is like a teacher and not a confession father. The layman does not give an absolution, and so you do not have to reveal to him everything. You are just taking guidance on specific matters, without mentioning that you have fallen into sin.

FORGIVENESS OF SINS:

After completing all the elements of confession, are all the sins forgiven no matter how horrible they were?

Of course!! The promises of God are true and so are the sayings of His saints. St. John says: "If we confess our sins, He is faithful and just to forgive us our sins and to cleanse us from all unrighteousness." (1 Jn 1:9).

St. John Chrysostom said: "If you have sinned, enter the church and wipe away your sins. Whenever you sin, offer repentance and do not lose hope of the promised grace. Even if you are in an old age, get inside and offer repentance because the church is a hospital and not a court. The church is not a place of judgement."

TIMES OF CONFESSION:

We are assuring again that a full confession is not

appropriate during the Holy Liturgy. It must be conducted in assigned times, so that you might have enough time.

INTERVALS OF CONFESSION:

As for the duration between each confession, this should be agreed upon with your confession father, according to your spiritual needs and circumstances. It should not be long period intervals.

PEOPLE OVERSEAS AND CONFESSION:

How would people overseas have confession if there is no Orthodox churches or Orthodox priests? These people should have a program of giving self-accounts, as well as being in contact with their confession fathers and sending letters containing their confession, till they meet any priest who can pray the Absolution prayer so that they gain the forgiveness of their sins.

SELF-EXAMINATION BEFORE CONFESSION

A proper full confession involves opening up completely with your confession father, without hiding any facts. Consequently, you have to examine yourself very honestly and accurately before confession. Here is a check list to help you examine yourself:

PRAYER:

1. Are you regular in your prayers or reluctant? If reluctant why? Are you always reluctant? Did you think about a solution? What was the result?

2. When do you pray? Morning? Before sleeping? Before and after eating? Before leaving home? Before doing anything? At any tribulation? Do you pray on the way? Do you pray while being with others?

3. Do you have special prayers where you talk for a long time with God? Are you regular? Is your prayer increasing or decreasing?

4. Do you pray all the Agpeya Prayers or just some? Which ones do you pray? If not, why?

5. Do you memorise Psalms and parts of the Agpeya? Is it increasing or decreasing? Do you use these Psalms and memorise them?

6. Is your prayer coming from a fervent heart? Are there tears sometimes? Do you feel the presence of God? Is your prayer lukewarm, or sometimes lukewarm and sometimes heartily? Why?

7. Are you sometimes absent minded during prayer? In which kinds of prayer are you absent minded? Does this last for a long time? How do you deal with this problem?

8. Do you stand and stretch your arms while praying? Do you kneel? Do you bow? Or do you have another position for prayer? Do you stand in respect before God? Or do you relax your feet? Do you lean towards the wall? Do you move your hands or look around?

9. Are there specific subjects that occupy your mind while praying? Do you pray for your sins and spiritual life? Do you pray for others? Do you pray for those who annoy you? Do you ask for materialistic things?

10. Do you give God time when you are fresh? Or do you pray while being tired and just give God the leftovers of your day?

FASTING:

1. Do you fast all the church fasting periods or just some of them? Which periods are regular? Do you fast weekly on Wednesdays and Fridays? Are there any obstacles facing your fasting? If so, what are they?

2. Do you abstain? For how long?

3. Do you crave certain dishes? Do you get filled with them? Do you ask for special meals?

4. Do you spend a lot of money generally buying food, especially food accessories? Do you eat between meals?

ALMSGIVING:

1. Are you honest in giving your tithes to God?

2. Do you just give your expected tithes or do you give abundantly ?

3. How do you feel about almsgiving? Do you feel proud or do you feel love towards the Lord's poor brethren?

4. Are you fed up with people asking for alms or do you give happily?

CONFESSION AND COMMUNION:

1. Are you having Holy Communion regularly? When was the last time?

2. Are you regular in confession? When was the last time?

3. If there is a shortage, what are the reasons?

4. Do you feel there is something you are hiding from your confession father?

5. Do you examine yourself properly and get ready before confession?

6. Are there any sins that you always confess yet keep falling into? What did you do to overcome them?

READING:

1. Do you read the Holy Bible regularly or randomly?

2. Do you meditate on whatever you read?

3. Do you have Bible studies? Do you read explanations for the Bible?

4. Do you read other spiritual books? Which kind (spiritualities, saints, doctrine...?) Are you regular in reading spiritual books?

5. Do you read other books? Do you read books that cause you to stumble?

6. On average, how many hours do you spend in religious readings daily or weekly?

7. Do you use your readings to improve your life style and spiritual practices?

PROSTRATIONS:

Do you perform prostrations? How many? Are you regular? Are they accompanied with short prayers?

GOING TO CHURCH:

1. Are you regular in going to church and attending the Holy Mass? If not, why?

2. Do you attend the Holy Mass while fasting or do you eat before going?

3. Do you go to church early or late? Do you attend all of the prayers, including vespers?

4. Do you attend other meetings apart from the Holy Liturgy: sermons, youth meetings, Sunday School...etc? Are you regular?

5. Do you serve at church? In which field? Are you honest in your service? Are you facing any problems, making you feel uncomfortable?

SPIRITUAL PRACTICES:

1. Do you have spiritual practices? What are they? Are you successful? If not, why?

2. Are there any virtues you want to practice?

YOUR RELATIONSHIP WITH OTHERS

1. Do you have a good relationship with elders, youth, family members, co-workers and the rest of the people? Do you have any problems with anyone? If so, what is it?

2. Are you angry with anyone? Who? Why?

3. Every time you are angry, is your anger suppressed or obvious? Is your voice loud? Do you yell? Do you say hurtful words? Do you insult others? Do you fight with people?

4. Do you calm down quickly or are you angry for a while? For how long? Do you have a hard time thinking about it? Does it leave anything in your heart against anyone? Is there any ruction for a while? Do you bear any grudge, hatred or enmity within your heart?

5. If you have ruction with anyone, do you make up or not? Do you take the first step towards reconciliation,

or does the other person take the first step? Does someone else intermediate? For how long do you bear the ruction? Is everything fine now?

6. Is there anyone who annoys or harms you? How do you deal with that person (within yourself and in public)?

7. What is the level of your tolerance? Long-suffering? Forgivness? Love of enemies?

8. Do you harm others through ignorance, forgetfullness or through a joke? What do you do about it? Do you apologise?

9. Do you harm others by justifying yourself and defending the truth? What kind of offence?

10.   Which obstacles hinder the virtue of meekness in your attitudes?

11.   Do you perform your duties towards everyone or are you sometimes falling short in family, work, church or general social relatioships?

12.   Do you have evil company? With who? What are the sins which you commit as a result? Do you have friends who drag you away from church and the love of God?

13.   Do you have a good financial relationship with others? Were you unjust to anyone? Did you cheat anyone? Did you sneak around anyone's rights or postpone them?

14.   Do you perform your financial duties towards God? What is the position of the virtue of almsgiving in your life (concerning tithes, first fruits and

participating in the church needs)?

15.   Do you deal with others humbly or proudly?

16.   Are you a sharp, harsh, hard-hearted person or a merciful one? Are you a lenient, weak person? What are the mistakes which you make consequently?

17.   Do you love other's praise? Do you look forward to it? How? How do you feel if someone vilified, ignored, opposed or treated you contrary to what you expect?

18.   Do you try to act in a certain way, other than what you really are?

19.   Does your attitude stumble anyone?

20.   Do you serve others and toil to make everyone happy? What is the situation of this virtue in your life?

SINS OF THE TONGUE:

1. What are the sins of the tongue which you commit? Do you insult, judge others, blaspheme, vow, swear, make fun of others, joke badly, partake of stupid conversations or any other inappropriate talking?

2. Who do you commit these sins with? Towards whom? How many times, as far as you can remember? Why do you sin this way? Is it a current habit?

3. Do you think about resisting these sins? How? What was the result?

4. Are you a talkative person? Do you talk about

every topic even if you don't know much about it? Do you feel that you are wasting time in excessive talking, speaking unnecessarily, while you could have used this time in profitable matters?

5. Do you sing worldly songs? Do you use words which are inappropriate for the children of God to use?

6. Do you talk in a wrong way? Is your voice loud? Sharp? Do you use body language a lot? Do you talk slowly or quickly? Do you think before talking? Do you hasten to speak rashly? Do you sometimes interrupt others? Do you go astray in your conversations with others?

7. Do you interfere in other people's business and force your opinion on them? Do you like instructing and rebuking others, even elders or foreigners, or people who wouldn't accept your view?

8. Do you practice silence? What is the result?

SINS OF THE MIND:

1. What are the sins of the mind which you commit? Adultery, anger, grudge, revenge, judging others, mistrust, pride, envy, daydreams, blaspheme, doubt, misunderstanding others… or any other desire?

2. Does the thought stay with you for a long time or does it go away quickly?

3. Does this thought come to you and you try to dismiss it, or do you welcome and enjoy it, adding more?

4. Does this thought turn into a desire, thus attracting you to carry on with the sin? Do you easily sin in mind

and sin in action?

5. Do you get occupied with the numerous worries of the world and its issues?

SINS OF THE SENSES:

1. What are the sins which you commit with your senses, especially looking, hearing and touching? Do you fall into adultery through touching? Do you desire things which are not yours? Do you spy on others? Do you enjoy listening to rude words and jokes?

SINS OF THE HEART:

1. What are the desires and emotions inside your heart? Do they displease God? Do you suffer from envy, jealousy, lust, hatred, love of riches or positions, love for the world, desires for materialistic possessions or desires for revenge?

2. Do you feel anger, murmur, fury, pain, despair or grief in your heart?

3. Do these desires and feelings appear in your practical life? Do they produce certain thoughts? Do you dream of them?

THE SINS OF ACTIONS:

1. What are the sins which you have already committed? In what way did you disobey the commandments of God? Was it adultery, stealing, killing, fighting?

2. How many times do you repeat the same sin? With whom and to whom?

3. What was the damage caused by your sin? Is the damage still there or have you removed the damage?

4. Are there any permanent reasons which lead you to sin or are they all temporary reasons? What did you do to avoid all of these reasons?

5. Did you try to repent and abandon these sins? Did you succeed or fail?

A REMARK:

All the questions mentioned above are to help beginners in fixing their spiritual life. It helps them be honest and accurate with themselves before confession.

However, those who are advanced in their spiritual life, have another responsibility. That is, to examine themselves positively, concerning Christian virtues which they are lacking.

We are all asked to live in holiness and perfection. We have to grow in grace and virtue, "but grow in the grace and knowledge of our Lord and Savior Jesus Christ." (2 Pet 3:18)

Thus those who are advanced spiritually should examine themselves from both sides; positively and negatively. This provides a motivation which keeps them growing in their holy life with the Lord.

PRAYERS BEFORE AND AFTER CONFESSION

A PRAYER BEFORE CONFESSION:

O Holy Father who awaits the return of sinners, You gave Your promise that You are ready to accept those who repent. Look now to a soul that was lost in the valleys of disobedience. For a long time I have tasted the bitterness of misery, being away from the stream of salvation. Now I come back to You to be purified, accept and do not reject me, for when You look at me with mercy and compassion, I will be cleansed and saved. If You turn away, I shall perish. Grant me O Lord, Your blessing to strengthen my will to come closer to You in faith and hope, to confess my sins and detest returning to them. May Your Holy Spirit remind me not to stray. May You enlighten my heart so I can see the graveness of my sins and negligence and have the will to obey Your commandments and live for the Glory of Your Holy Name. Amen.

A PRAYER AFTER CONFESSION:

O' Father, I am grateful for Your goodness, and love for mankind. You did not wish that I perish, but awakened me from my sleep and guided me to Your path. You saved me from the valley of death to the protection of Your strong fortress. Fill me with hope and faith. I come to You like the sick wishing to be healed, like the hungry seeking to be filled, like the thirsty to the springs of living water, like the poor to the source of riches and the sinner to the redeemer and like the dying to the origin of life. You are my salvation, my health, my life and my strength. With You, I find consolation, happiness and comfort. Help me, protect me and surround me with Your goodness. Teach me to put my will in Your hands and live according to Your will. Remove my weakness so I may be firm and honest to You to the end. Amen.

Holy Communion

꘎

"He who eats My flesh and drinks My blood
abides in Me, and I in him."
(Jn 6: 56)

- ❧ What is Holy Communion?
- ❧ The honour of this Mystery
- ❧ How do we benefit from this Holy Mystery?
- ❧ General information about Holy Communion.
- ❧ Questions and Answers
- ❧ Prayers before and after Holy Communion

WHAT IS HOLY COMMUNION?

IT IS A COVENANT:

Holy Communion is a Covenant between God and His people, by which He becomes their God and they become His children. "Likewise He also took the cup after supper, saying, "This cup is the new covenant in My blood, which is shed for you." (Luke 22: 20). St. Paul talks about this Covenant: "Behold, the days are coming, says the Lord, when I will make a new covenant with the house of Israel and with the house of Judah not according to the covenant that I made with their fathers in the day when I took them by the hand to lead them out of the land of Egypt; because they did not continue in My covenant, and I disregarded them, says the Lord. For this is the covenant that I will make with the house of Israel after those days, says the Lord: I will put My laws in their mind and write them on their hearts; and I will be their God, and they shall be My people. None of them shall teach his neighbor, and none his brother, saying, 'Know the Lord,' for all shall know Me, from the least of them to the greatest of them. For I will be merciful to their unrighteousness, and their sins and their lawless deeds I will remember no more." (Heb 8: 8-12)

IT IS CHURCH MEMBERSHIP:

It is membership in the church community, i.e. we are all members in the Body of Christ, which is the church.

St. Paul says: "The cup of blessing which we bless, is it not the communion of the blood of Christ? The bread which we break, is it not the communion of the body of Christ? For we, though many, are one bread and one body; for we all partake of that one bread." (1 Cor 10:16–17). Thus, believers partake of Holy Communion to be in one covenant with each other, united in One Body, "And if one member suffers, all the members suffer with it; or if one member is honored, all the members rejoice with it." (1 Cor 12: 26).

In the Liturgy of St. Basil, the church prays "Make us all worthy, O our Master, to partake of Your holies, unto the purification of our souls, our bodies and our spirits, that we become one body and one spirit…"

A SPIRITUAL GRACE FOR GODLINESS:

It is a great spiritual grace, granting us the grace of living, abiding and growing in a miraculous way that surpasses all other means. The church expresses this fact in the Fraction: "He instituted for us this great mystery of godliness…."

Holy Communion is truly a Mystery of Godliness!!

THE HONOUR OF THIS MYSTERY

The gifts and blessings of the Lord are numerous. His power is so mighty and His love is so deep. In the Holy Liturgy of St. Gregory, the Theologian we pray: "Holy, Holy, Holy are You, O Lord and Holy in everything, and most excellent is the light of Your essence, and inexpressible is the power of Your wisdom. No manner of speech is able to define the depth of Your love for mankind."

St. John Chrysostom says: "People usually yearn to see the Lord; what He looks like and what He wears, but what you are seeing, touching and eating now is the Lord Himself. He is giving you Himself. Although you cannot gaze on Him because of His glory and light, you can eat Him and be united with Him."

All the works of God are full of glory and grandeur, but the Mystery of the Holy Eucharist is the pinnacle of His glory and grandeur. The Lord granted us spiritual weapons with which we can fight and conquer (Eph 6: 11- 16), of which Holy Communion is considered the strongest and toughest weapon.

It is no wonder that Holy Communion is considered the strongest weapon because it is a continuation of the atoning sacrifice of the Cross, through which the Only Begotten Son of God gave Himself on behalf of the entire world. He crushed Satan, broke the thorn of death and defeated Hades.

St. Macarius the Great says: "You conquer the enemies with this great Mystery; he who belittles It, will be defeated by the powers of darkness."

Through Holy Communion, we conquer the reasons behind sin, especially the inner desires, the attacks of the devils and the attractions of the world. That's why the Church calls Holy Communion 'The Food of the Mighty'. This is absolutely true, for we are partaking of that about which is written, "And the whole multitude sought to touch Him, for power went out from Him and healed them all." (Lk 6: 19)

St. John Chrysostom says: "Let the sick partake of it in faith, for those who used to touch His hem were healed. How about us who are taking and eating Him?", also "Let us be like the lions blazing with the fire of love and terrifying the devils after partaking of this Holy Mystery."

St. Ambrose says: "Let the Lord Jesus be a Guest for your soul. If Jesus is there, then peace is present. When the devils see that Guest Jesus closing the doors of temptations, you will be safe and able to spend your life peacefully."

Our spiritual weapons get power from the Divine Grace of the Body and Blood of the Lord Christ. We fight our enemies with many spiritual weapons, but with this specific weapon of Holy Communion, the Lord Jesus Himself is defeating our enemies. He says; "He who eats My flesh and drinks My blood abides in Me, and I in him." (Jn 6:56), and St. Paul also says, "it is no longer I who live, but Christ lives in me." (Gal 2:20)

When we conquer our enemies, it is actually the Blood of Christ which is conquering. We see this in the Book of Revelation, "And they overcame him (Satan) by the blood of the Lamb (Christ)." David the Prophet also says: "You prepare a table before me in the presence of my enemies;" (Ps 23:5) Holy Communion is the Holy Table prepared by the Lord to strengthen us in defeating our spiritual enemies.

Partaking of the Holy Body and Precious Blood of the Lord is food for our life and spirit. It is the food prepared by the Lord to those who fear Him, as interpreted by the early fathers regarding Psalm 111: 4,5 "He has made His wonderful works to be remembered; The Lord is gracious and full of compassion. He has given food to those who fear Him; He will ever be mindful of His covenant."

St. Augustine cried out saying: "O You, the Mystery of Goodness, the Trait of Unity, the Bond of Love. He who wants to live with You and gain life, let him partake of Your Body and live forever."

The children of Israel ate manna for forty years in the wilderness till they reached the Promised Land (the Earthly Jerusalem). Similarly, the Eurcharist feeds our souls and protects us in the world till we reach the Heavenly Jerusalem.

The Lord made several promises when He established the Mystery of the Eucharist.

"He who eats My flesh and drinks My blood abides in Me, and I in him." How does this work? Nobody can comprehend it. However, we know and trust in the blessings of this Mystery and in the abiding relationship that forms between Man and God when we partake of it.

The Lord Jesus says: "I am the vine, you are the branches. He who abides in Me, and I in him, bears much fruit; for without Me you can do nothing. If anyone does not abide in Me, he is cast out as a branch and is withered; and they gather them and throw them into the fire, and they are burned. If you abide in Me, and My words abide in you, you will ask what you desire, and it shall be done for you." (Jn 15: 5-7)

So through partaking of Holy Communion, the believer

abides in Christ and Christ in him. We can repeat with St. Paul; "...that their hearts may be encouraged, being knit together in love, and attaining to all riches of the full assurance of understanding, to the knowledge of the mystery of God, both of the Father and of Christ, in whom are hidden all the treasures of wisdom and knowledge." (Col 2:2-3)

The following are meditations regarding the Lord's promises.

When You came down in Your glory on Mount Sinai, the Mountain quaked, thundered and was covered in smoke. You told Moses, 'Take heed to yourselves that you do not go up to the mountain or touch its base. Whoever touches the mountain shall surely be put to death. Not a hand shall touch him, but he shall surely be stoned or shot with an arrow; whether man or beast, he shall not live.' (Ex 19: 12-13) At this, Moses was terrified and trembled.

In the Old Testament they wouldn't dare touch the mountain where You descended in Your Glory; while in the New Testament, the priest carries You in his hands and we all eat You in order to abide and live in You!

How could this Fire which consumes the evil ones, be a fire for our purification, burning all the weeds of evil within us and blazing our hearts with Your love?

The blessings of this Holy Mystery also affect our eternal life.

The Lord of Glory says: "I am the living bread which came down from heaven. If anyone eats of this bread, he will live forever; and the bread that I shall give is My flesh, which I shall give for the life of the world."

"Whoever eats My flesh and drinks My blood has eternal life, and I will raise him up at the last day. For My flesh is food indeed, and My blood is drink indeed. He who eats My flesh and drinks My blood abides in Me, and I in him." (Jn 6: 51-56)

St. Cyril, the pillar of the faith, says: "He gave us His True Body and Blood to waive the power of corruption and for the dwelling of the Holy Spirit within us. In this way, we have companionship with His Holiness and we become spiritual people, higher than those in heaven."

Everytime you partake of Holy Communion, you are accepting the Lord into your heart to purify, bless and clean you. He entered into the womb of St. Mary, making her the Queen of the heavenlies and the earthlies. He entered Zachariah's house, filling John with the Holy Spirit, even though still in Elizabeth's womb. He entered the manger, turning it into a sanctuary and a paradise for angels and humans. He entered Egypt, making all idols fall down. He entered Jordan and sanctified its waters. He entered Peter's house and healed his mother-in-law. He entered Jairus' house and raised his daughter from death. He entered Zaccheus' house and justified him. He entered Mary and Martha's house, making them saints.

If we can preserve fruits and vegetables for a long period of time, doesn't the Holy Body and Blood of Lord Jesus preserve our life from the roots of sin?

HOW TO BENEFIT FROM THIS MYSTERY

People usually ask: "Why don't we feel the blessings of this Mystery when we approach It?"

The answer is: You are not preparing yourself adequately for this Holy Mystery.

Noah toiled 100 years in building an Ark, through which he saved a few people. Solomon spent 7 years building the House of God after which he spent 8 days celebrating its construction and offering 1000 sacrifices. While we do not spend a single hour getting ready for this Wonderful Grace!!

There are several spiritual practices which can help us prepare for Holy Communion. It is better to start them on the eve of the previous day. These practices should be in accordance with regularly repentance, confession and self-examination.

FIRST PREPARE YOURSELF EMOTIONALLY:

It is now the eve of the day of Communion. Sit quietly and think about your holy yearnings towards your Beloved Lord Jesus Christ, Who is giving you Himself in this Holy Mystery. The more you get ready, the more you will feel the comfort and blessings of God filling your heart.

When the disciples asked the Lord Jesus"Where do You want us to go and prepare, that You may eat the

Passover?" He guided two of them to ".....a large upper room, furnished and prepared" (Mk 14: 12, 15). The Lord Jesus Himself chose the place to eat the Passover with His disciples, and there He established the Glorious Mystery of the Eucharist. The place which He chose was a "large upper room, furnished and prepared", which has a remarkable significance…

The upper room, which is the highest place in a house, denotes sublimity. In the incident of Transfiguration, when Jesus wanted to show His three disciples His glory, He took them to a high mountain (Mk 9: 2). Similarly, anyone who wants to touch the Glory of the Lord, has to reach a high level of meditation.

The upper room was furnished and prepared. Consequently, the Lord wants our hearts to be ready and ornamented with virtues, prepared to accept Him. If someone of high prestige is walking by, we clean the streets and take away all rubbish. How much more should we clean our hearts of the dirt of sin and ornament it with feelings of love and contrition, for Christ who is about to dwell inside?

Our Lord wants you to partake of the Holy Mystery and prepare a place for Him in your heart, so that He might get united with you, help you in your fights and dismiss all your earthly desires. We cannot comprehend why our Lord wants to be united with us, but we do know that He loves us. He expressed this love in His words, "… and my delight was with the sons of men." (Prov 8: 31)

In offering us this Glorious Mystery, God is giving up His glory by turning Himself into Food to satisfy our souls, about which He says: "Blessed are those who hunger and thirst for righteousness, For they shall be filled." (Mt 5:6). In doing this, He is saving our souls and uniting Himself with us. So how do we prepare ourselves to accept Him?

If Moses constructed the Ark of Covenant out of wood which does not rot and coated it in pure gold, in order to place the Tablets of the Law, how about the human soul wherein God will come and abide? It should be void of the rot of sin and ornamented with Divine Virtues!!

Joseph of Arimathea, honoured the Body of Our Saviour and buried Him in a brand new tomb, where no one else had been buried before. How could we then, dare to accept the Lord Jesus in a heart where envy, jealousy and the love of the world have been buried before? How can we dare take Christ inside a heart that smells with bad desires and intentions?

Beware of approaching this Feast without being ready and without wearing the appropraite Wedding gown (Mt 22: 1-14). The Lord Jesus rose Jairus' daughter from the dead, then gave her something to eat. You too, must repent and rise up from the death of sin, then approach this Heavenly Food. The manna, with which the children of Israel were fed in the wilderness, was a signal of His Holy Body and Precious Blood. We too, in the wilderness of this world, have to be fed with the Spiritual Manna.

The manna was not given to the children of Israel except after their exodus from Egypt (Land of Slavery) and their crossing of the Red Sea. Similarly, no one can accept this Spiritual Food before being liberated from the spiritual Pharaoh (i.e. Satan), and going through the sea of repentance.

SECOND: MEDITATE ON THE UTMOST LOVE OF GOD:

Think and meditate on the love of God as revealed to you in this Great Mystery. God not only created you in His likeness and sent His Only Begotten Son to save and restore you to your original rank, but also gave you His Body and Blood as a nurture and cure for your spiritual sicknesses.

Think deeply and question yourself: "When did God start loving me? Is it the same time I started loving Him or did He love me ever since I was an embryo?"

God loved you much before that. He loved you before you entered the world. He loved you before He created the world.

As a pregnant mother prepares everything for the arrival of her baby, it is the same with the love of God. He prepared every spiritual means for you before your birth, "Yes, I have loved you with an everlasting love; therefore with lovingkindness I have drawn you." (Jer 31: 3)

The love of God is implied through our Salvation and Redemption. He gave us an eternal promise, to be with Him until the very end (Matt. 28: 30). His presence with us doesn't only mean taking care of us, but rather, abiding with us. Through Holy Communion, He is present with us, in the form of His Body and Blood. How wonderful is the name 'Emmanuel' which means 'God is with us'.

The great power of God is revealed through the creation of the world, and in this Mystery, His utmost love is declared. Ahasuerus, king of Persia had a banquet for six months and invited all the nobels and princes, as written in Esther 1. Without a doubt, it was the biggest news of the world at the time. Yet could Ahasuerus' feast be compared to that of the Lord Jesus Christ, which lasted for 2000 years and will continue through till the end of the world?

Ahasuerus offered an earthly meal, while our Lord offered Himself. This is a very unique event as we have never heard of anyone feeding himself to his children. On the contrary, we have heard of mothers killing their children and eating them during times of famine!!

If we meditate on the great love of God, we will find that He established this great Mystery at a time when people were plotting to kill Him. At a time when the carpenter was preparing the cross, and the blacksmith preparing the nails. Despite all this, the Lord Jesus was preparing the Food of Life for humanity.

THIRD: MEDITATE ON HIS WONDEROUS HUMILITY:

God showed us His great love through humility. St Jerome says: "How humble You are, my Master, You come to a sinner and accept to be eaten by him and to unite with him!!"

Meditating on the Lord's humility will help you gain humility within yourselves. He ordered us to imitate Him, "Learn from Me, for I am gentle and lowly in heart" (Mt 11: 29). If God, the Mighty and Powerful had humbled Himself to lift me up, shouldn't I humble myself to be worthy of His dwelling within me?

How humble are You my Master? The heavens are not pure before Your eyes and You are calling me, the sinner, to come close to You, to eat Your Body and be united with

You!! Who would believe these words unless You uttered them O My Lord?!

When Your pure mother visited Elizabeth, the latter said in humbleness, "But why is this granted to me, that the mother of my Lord should come to me?" (Lk 1: 43) How would I feel when I am about to accept the Creator and Redeemer of St. Mary??

The pagan centurion felt unworthy that Jesus would go into his house and heal his servant, "Lord, I am not worthy that You should come under my roof. But only speak a word, and my servant will be healed." (Mt 8: 8)

What about me? I am the one who knew the Truth, was enlighted with the Grace, tasted the Heavenly gifts and the Good Word of God and became a partner of the Holy Spirit?

FOURTH: SOME PRATICES BEFORE AND AFTER HOLY COMMUNION:

Spiritual Practices should be done the day before you partake of Holy Communion. It is preferable to go to bed early so that you can wake up early and fresh. If you wake up during midnight for any reason, recite some verses. The Lord smells these words as a sweet aroma.

In the morning:

Before going to church, think about the number of times you have stepped away from God ever since you last partook of Holy Communion. Remember that you had disgraced your God by falling into sin. Give Him all your sins and desires, for he bears the sins of the whole world. Don't be disturbed, but rather fill your heart with hope because of the Grace you are about to partake. Approach the Lord in humility and prepare your heart so that He may come and rest.

On your way to church, try to keep your heart and mind on the Great Mystery you are about to partake of. Recite the Psalms that are usually prayed for the occasion, and blaze your heart with the love of God.

During the Holy Liturgy:

Stand in a quiet spot at church so that your thoughts are not interrupted. When you are just about to partake of Holy Communion, think deeply and humbly: Who are you to share in this great Mystery? Who is Jesus, who is about to dwell inside your heart? Jesus is the Son of the Great God, of Whom the heaven and all its powers tremble. He is the Holy of Holies. He is the Almighty Lord!

Think of yourself; Who are you?

You are nothing. You are worse than other creatures and beasts because of your sins and iniquities. Instead of giving thanks to your Great God and Creator, you belittle His Precious Blood which was shed for your sake (Heb 10:9). Yet still He calls you to partake of His Banquet because of His everlasting and unchangeable love for you. More so, He encourages you to partake of this Royal Mystery, because He is FULL of Love. He never closes the door of His mercy, even if you are lying in the depth of sin.

However, He does mention the consequences of rejecting His mercy, "Then Jesus said to them, "Most assuredly, I say to you, unless you eat the flesh of the Son of Man and drink His blood, you have no life in you." (Jn 6:53).

The Awesome Moment:

After fortifying yourself with His mercy and getting warmed with His love, approach the Holy Communion in fear, awe and reverence saying:

"O Lord, I am not worthy to partake of this Holy Mystery, as I frequently disappointed You with my numerous sins. I am full of hypocrisy and iniquity. I haven't submitted myself totally and honestly to Your love. O Almighty Lord, through Your mercy and love, make me worthy to accept You, for I have come in faith and hope."

When you open your mouth for the Holy Body, say to the priest "I have sinned my father, absolve me", then in total faith, hope and love, after having the Holy Body, cover your mouth as if hiding a precious treasure (Matthew 13), or as if hiding this Great Mystery in your heart so that you might not sin against the Lord, resembling David the Prophet; "I hid Your words in my heart so that I might not sin against You".

After Partaking of Holy Communion:

At Church: After having a sip of water, stay in a quiet

spot, close the doors of your inner self and forget all about your surroundings. Pray to God saying:

"O Almighty God, Creator of heaven and earth, what made You dwell in my unworthy heart? I am poor, blind and naked! It is Your unexpressable love! What do You want O Lord from Your poor slave? I know you need nothing except my love towards You. You want no other fire to blaze my heart except the fire of Your love which consumes all other ungodly desires. Now Lord, listen to the vows of my heart: Look at me, tie my will to Yours, my desire to Yours! As You have given me Yourself totally, I am also giving You myself. I cannot do this by myself, but with You I can do everything."

After the priest dismisses the congregation, do not rush outside the church, lest you meet relatives or friends and start talking about unuseful issues or silly jokes. Rather, wait inside the church for a short time until everyone has left. Try to make use of the Grace you just partook of. Store spiritual things that will be of a benefit when you are lukewarm in spirit. We advise you to have Communion on a day during which you are not too busy. For example, we don't recommend you to have Holy Communion in an early Mass if you are going straight to work, unless there is a need to do so. As part of the church's holy wisdom, you cannot spit or take something out of your mouth after partaking of Holy Communion. This is to remind you of the Holy Grace, which you have just partook of.

At Home

Go home straight away, and if possible, do not get

engaged in any physical or worldly activity. Of course here, we are not talking about your church service or study committments. Try to spend some time alone and do not eat immediately. Lift your heart in prayers to thank God for this Grace and ask Him to protect you from reluctancy and leniency. You will have a better chance at home, after Communion, to talk to the Lord about your emotions and pleadings.

Be aware that the devil is following you and threading nets for your fall. However, always ignore any trifle reason for frustration. You have gained an abundant Grace and a fiery weapon. Try to use Holy Communion in strengthening your faith, holiness and piety, "Blessed are those who believe without seeing" (Jn 20:29).

St. Paul says; "For as often as you eat this bread and drink this cup, you proclaim the Lord's death till He comes." (1 Cor 11: 26) St. Basil the Great explains the duties of a person who has partaken of Holy Communion: "The Son of Man tolerated sufferings and death for the sake of all humanity and for all those who partake of His Holy Body and Blood."

"He died for all, that those who live should live no longer for themselves, but for Him who died for them and rose again." (2 Cor 5:15). Thus, all those who partake of Holy Communion should not be ready to live for themselves or for the world, but according to the Lord's commandments and will.

Beware of joining the Jews who welcomed the Lord on Palm Sunday crying, "Hosanna to the Son of David" and few days later, shouted out to crucify Him!! Be honest and faithful in your love to the Lord; ask Him to strengthen you and to protect the clean and pure robe you've just worn.

GENERAL INFORMATION ABOUT HOLY COMMUNION

REGULAR PARTAKING OF HOLY COMMUNION:

If Holy Communion is such a sublime, blessed and effective means, among all other spiritual practices, then we should yearn and be fully prepared to regularly partake of It as a "purification for our souls, bodies and spirits." My dear brethren, nothing should prevent you. The Banquet is close to you and it is for free. However, it is your choice and responsibility to prepare for this amazing Mystery.

All believers should regularly partake of Holy Communion. The only thing necessary is spiritual preparation, a state which we are all supposed to be continually practicing. Early Christians used to attend the Holy Liturgy and partake of Holy Communion on a weekly basis.

St. Paul writes about the early church; "And they continued steadfastly in the apostles' doctrine and fellowship, in the breaking of bread, and in prayers." (Acts 2: 42). Thus, we have to have Holy Communion weekly, fortnightly or at least once every month.

Some people claim that partaking of Holy Communion frequently causes us to belittle the honour of this Holy Sacrament. In response, we say that spiritual preparation preceeding this Sacrament, inflames our spirituality and adds to our reverence. If this claim was true, then we have to refrain from praying for a while, but on the contrary, the more we pray, the more we grow in love towards God. Remember that the Bible orders us to pray without ceasing (Luke 18: 1, 1 Thes. 5: 17)

Partaking of Holy Communion on Occasions only:
Some Christians partake in Holy Communion on specific occasions only, such as Maundy Thursday or Joyous Saturday. We do not object these holy days, but we disagree with the fact that people choose to have Communion only on specific occasions. We have to have Holy Communion regularly, in order to keep our divine covenant with the Lord.

According to church tradition, an engaged couple should have Holy Communion before their wedding ceremony. The whole point is to offer pure confession and repentance before completing the Sacrament of Marriage. This minimises marital problems and any other unpleasant result.

We advise engaged couples to practice proper repentance and confession. They must remember that church traditions are not dry routines but are full of life and spirit.

THE MEANING OF BEING WORTHY OF COMMUNION:

Lots of people refrain from Holy Communion out of fear of undeservedness, especially after hearing the priest pray in the Holy Liturgy: "Make us all worthy our Master to partake of Your Holies, as purification for our souls, bodies and spirits," Furthermore, "The Holies are for the holy people." The deacon also says: "Pray for being worthy to partake of these Holy Sacraments."

So, how do we prepare ourselves for this Holy Sacament? Is it to be without sin? Is it to purify ourselves from any evil whatsoever?

Our personal efforts will never make us perfect, no matter how hard we try. It is the work of Divine Grace which helps us, as St. Paul says: "I do not set aside the grace of God; for if righteousness comes through the law, then Christ died in vain." (Gal 2: 21). Refraining from Holy Communion until we become perfect means that we depend on our own power. On the contrary, we should resort to the Lord with all our weaknesses and shortages so that He might perfect us. We know that the Prodigal Son came back to his father with his dirty clothes, and his father was the one who clothed him with the best robe and shoes. It was the Father who gave him the ring of his hand!!

It is the same with us; we cannot be pure and clean unless we return to our Heavenly Father. Being worthy for Communion means to approach this Mystery in awe, reverence and honour, while feeling unworthy. It is similar to a patient who takes medications to cure his ailments and pains. The priest says "The Holies are for the holy people." God understands our unworthy state and He knows that the Only Holy One is Jesus Christ Who incarnated for our salvation. Consequrntly, the congregation responds "One is the Holy Father, One is the Holy Son, One is the Holy Spirit Amen."

St. Paul warns those who approach Holy Communion

reluctantly, "For he who eats and drinks in an unworthy manner eats and drinks judgment to himself, not discerning the Lord's body." (1 Cor 11:29) He targets the same issue in this verse: "But let a man examine himself, and so let him eat of the bread and drink of the cup." (1 Cor 11: 28)

St. John Chrysostom writes: "Never approach Holy Communion reluctantly, but let us all approach in enthusiasm because the punishment is not a trifle one. Beware of being a criminal towards the Body and Blood of the Lord Christ."

Out of human weakness, we sometimes fall into our same old sins and iniquities after all our vows with God, but do not be afraid or let down. Always remember St. John's words; "My little children, these things I write to you, so that you may not sin. And if anyone sins, we have an Advocate with the Father, Jesus Christ the righteous. And He Himself is the propitiation for our sins, and not for ours only but also for the whole world." (1 Jn 2: 1-2)

NECESSARY PHYSICAL PURITY:

Partaking of Holy Communion necessitates cleanness and purity of the body as well as the spirit:

1. In the case of wet dreams, males should refrain from Holy Communion because it is considered a breaking of the fast. If wet dreams are frequently occurring, it should be revealed to the confession father, as sometimes it is a devilish war to prevent someone from partaking of the Holy Mystery. The confession father can then guide to an appropriate decision.

2. Females should refrain from Holy Communion during their periods and after giving birth; The mother refrains for 40 days for baby boys and 80 days for baby girls.

3. There should be no intimate relationship between husband and wife on the eve of Holy Communion as this is considered breaking the fast.

4. Communion should be approached with a clean bathed body; even the clothes should be free of any traces of wet dreams or the like.

THE RELATIONSHIP BETWEEN THE PRIEST AND THIS MYSTERY:

Some people refrain from Holy Communion as a result of the priest's wickedness, weaknesses or faults. Yet despite this, they don't even put any effort into changing the priest. They generalise their judgment and follow the devil's trick which prevents them from receiving the great blessings of this mystery.

The question here: Is there is any relationship between the piety of the priest and the completion of this Mystery? Should the priest be saintly so that the bread and wine turn into the Holy Body and Precious Blood of Lord Jesus?

The servant priest should have strong faith, piety and holiness befitting this Honourable Mystery, yet the power and grace of the Mystery is not related to the servant priest or his piety. It is all related to the will of our Saviour, the Giver of grace. It is a result of the vital Divine words, "This is My Body, This is My Blood. Do this in remembrance of Me." This is the case with all Seven

Mysteries of the church. They do not take place because of the piety of the priests, but because of the descent of the Holy Spirit through their prayers, thus the priests are just visible instruments through which God performs His Mysteries.

Consequently, God does not put a condition of holiness on the human being to deliver His Grace to His children; otherwise this would lead to great confusion in the church of Christ.

In addition, a righteous priest serving today could turn into a wicked one tomorrow and vice versa, because of the free will granted to him like everyone else. Thus God is the Only One Who knows the inner heart of everyone.

In a sermon about Baptism, St. Gregory the Theologian says: "You have to believe that he who has taken the authority of priesthood (but not one of the heretics who are excommunicated by the church) can purify you. One priest could excel over another in his spiritual life, but the power of Baptism is the same."

St John the Baptist witnessed the Lord Jesus through baptism, "This is He who baptizes with the Holy Spirit," (Jn 1:33) corresponding with, "though Jesus Himself did not baptize, but His disciples." (Jn 4:2) St Augustine comments about this: "If Peter or Paul or Jude were baptising, it is the same Jesus Christ Who is baptising because it is written 'This is He who baptises...'"

This is emphasised by St. Paul's words, "So then neither he who plants is anything, nor he who waters, but God who gives the increase." (1 Cor 3:7) Therefore, any power and effectiveness in the Mystery, is that of Christ.

The priest is just serving and he cannot resist the power of God.

Again, in his third book he writes: "There is no difference if the priest is a sinful or righteous one. Exactly like a farmer who is spreading the seeds, it doesn't matter if his hands are clean or dirty, the seeds will still give forth fruits. If the power of the Mysteries are related to the righteousness or wickedness of the priests, then our own salvation depends on their free will."

In conclusion, we have to believe that the priests are just tools through which the Lord Jesus is completing the Mysteries of His Holy Spirit. We don't have to doubt the truth or effectiveness of this Mystery, just because a "wicked" priest is performing the liturgy. Let's approach Holy Communion in faith and thanksgiving, always remembering the Lord's kindness and mercy, for He has established this Great Mystery for our righteous sake.

QUESTIONS AND ANSWERS

FASTING AND COMMUNION:

It is noted that some priests prevent those who are not fasting (whatever the reasons are), from partaking of Holy Communion. Is this appropriate?

Actually, this is an unappropriate ban because our Holy Church waives fasting for sick people, elderly people, pregnant women and nursing mothers. Consequently, if the church gives them an absolution not to fast, how can the Church then prevent them from Holy Communion? Only those who are punished by the church can be banned from Holy Communion. Also, if someone's spiritual status does not befit Holy Communion, they can be prevented. However, if someone is not fasting for any reason, they must receive an absolution from the priest.

In conclusion, no priest should prevent a believer from partaking in Holy Communion if he/she is not fasting any of the general church fasts.

DURATION OF PRECAUTION:

The term 'precaution' refers to the period preceeding Holy Communion, where we stop eating and drinking for nine hours. How about afternoon Masses such as those during Holy Lent? Can we eat in the morning and then fast for nine hours?

Definitely not. Our day starts from midnight, thus we should be fasting from midnight up until the partaking of the Mystery. The nine hours should be watched carefully for masses held very early such as Joyous Saturday, Christmas, Easter Midnight Masses and the like.

As for the precaution after Holy Communion, we should not spit or take anything out of our mouths.

FASTING AND CORRECT BELIEF:

Is it permissable for those that have deviated from the Orthodox doctrine to partake of Holy Communion in Orthodox Churches?

Definitely not, and the church should be aware and cautious of this. It is a fatally critical issue and the church should practice its authority on whoever deviates from the Orthodox doctrine.

Can any orthodox person partake of Holy Communion in a non-Orthodox church if they are overseas and there is no other available church?

No. The church should meet the needs of these orthodox congregations overseas and provide an orthodox service for them.

PRAYERS BEFORE AND AFTER COMMUNION

PRAYER BEFORE COMMUNION:

Lord, I am not worthy to have You come under my roof because I am a sinner, but only say the word; "Your sins are forgiven" and my soul will be healed. I am barren and empty of any goodness, I have nothing but Your compassion, mercy and love to mankind. You descended from your Heavenly Glory to our humility and consented to be born in a Manger. O' Holy Saviour, do not reject my humble and miserable soul which is waiting for Your Glorified coming. As You did not refuse to enter the leper's house to heal him. Please Lord, come into my soul to cleanse it. As You did not stop the adulteress from kissing Your feet, please do not prevent me from coming near You to receive Your Holy Body and Your Sacred Blood. May this Holy Communion banish every corruption and mortify all my evil desires. Help me to obey Your commandments and heal my soul and my body from every sin. May Your spirit dwell with in me and make me united with You so I may live for the Glory of Your Name. Amen.

PRAYER AFTER COMMUNION:

My tonge praises and my soul glorifies the Lord. My heart rejoices for You have come to me, Lord, and dressed me in purity and allowed me to Your feast. May my union with You today be everlasting, through it I grow in strength of faith and hope. Let my communion be a symbol of the grace of Your salvation, let it be a purification to my body and my soul and preparation for the everlasting love and joy. To You Lord, I surrender myself and my will, call to You my senses and bless them and let my mind to be according to Your will. Enlighten my heart, awaken my conscience, cast away all shadows of evil, hush the storms, walk with me and guide me. Give me comfort, quench my thirst, look with love at all my short comings, abide with me for the day is coming to an end and stay with me for a new day. You alone are my aim and happiness, now and forever. Amen

www.ingramcontent.com/pod-product-compliance
Lightning Source LLC
LaVergne TN
LVHW091306080426
835510LV00007B/383